# Our Blessed Mother

*Model of Faith, Humility and Courage*

May God Bless
all
The Sullivans!

# Our Blessed Mother

*Model of Faith, Humility and Courage*

**MIKE SULLIVAN**

gatekeeper press™

Tampa, Florida

Our Blessed Mother: Model of Faith, Humility and Courage

Published by Gatekeeper Press
7853 Gunn Hwy, Suite 209
Tampa, FL 33626
www.GatekeeperPress.com



ISBN (paperback): 9781662932960

# Table of Contents

Dedicated to All the Unknown Mothers
Who Died Bringing Life into the World

# Preface

On my coffee cup, there is an old Irish Blessing that goes like this:

*May your troubles be less, and your blessings be more, and may nothing but happiness come through your door.*

I like this saying. It puts me in a happy place. I do think about my blessings—my faith, my family, and the life God has given to me.

You cannot give faith to anyone—only God can accomplish this miracle. But you can share your faith and by doing so, you may bring someone closer to discovering the truth. I have tried to share my faith with my family and friends most of my life. It is very important to me that I share my faith with my grandchildren.

Eventually, we all become a picture on a family wall that will be forgotten someday. People will look at the picture and say, "Who was that?" If we are lucky, someone will say a kind word or two about us. Maybe not.

Life comes at you fast! When you are young, it is as if you are on that slow train like the one in the child's book, *The Little Engine That Could*. Days seem to last forever, especially summers. You just chug along. Nothing seems to matter, other than playtime with your friends and trying to stay out of trouble with your parents. Things are simple and uncomplicated. It is one big adventure; at least that is what I remember about my childhood.

As you age, the train speeds up like a fast-moving freight train. You can't jump off. You must hang on and ride it to its destination. You must hope for the best, and have faith that everything will work out in the end. In life, you face many emotional, financial, physical, and spiritual challenges that at times can seem overwhelming. If you just hang on and have faith in God, the ride will be easier and end well. Pretty simple stuff, right?

Today many of us see the world as broken. We seem to be lost. The world was not designed that way by the Creator, but we mortals have managed to really mess things up through our pride, selfishness, anger, and sinful ways. We are now involved in a struggle for the souls of our children and grandchildren. Forces are at play today to crush the family as well as our faith. Without faith, hope dies a slow death.

In many ways, our secular world has turned things upside down. If you are up for no consequences, earthly pleasures and delights, and a world where there are no norms, the current state of our world will probably suit you well. If, on the other hand, you believe in the promises of our Lord and in salvation, you will be challenged by the onslaught of evil that seems to have been magnified in recent years. Evil is, by its very nature, designed to break your will and spirit. Without faith, our souls will be dragged down to a place of great despair. Oh, that is just a bunch of malarkey, as some would say! Maybe? But I am betting that what we do here on Earth has eternal consequences.

I am not a scholar or overly religious. I have had my fair share of bad behavior in my life. I have stumbled, fallen, and gotten back up many times during my life. I consider myself ordinary. I am prideful and have a hard time being humble. I will defend what I believe to be the truth, and I disdain bullies and people who go out of their way to hurt others. I was blessed with average intelligence and a really bad temper.

I am a husband, a father, and a grandfather. I was raised Catholic and rediscovered the fullness of my faith after my son's death in 2017. I am blessed to have a wife who has supported me for over fifty years, three beautiful children, and eight wonderful grandchildren. The Lord has been good to me and our family.

I have tried to remain in friendship with the Lord throughout my life. I know what failure feels like, and I have made my share of mistakes. But I like to think I am not a quitter. I would like to think, on balance, I have put enough points on the board to get a crack at Heaven. I may have a stop along the way, but I feel closer to our Lord and his Blessed Mother today more than at any other time of my life. I think most of my feelings emanate from the fact that I do not have a lot of time left on my clock.

We are each unique in the eyes of our Creator. He gives each of us special gifts. Some are better than others at connecting at the spiritual level. My views of the Blessed Mother were greatly influenced by my Catholic upbringing, especially by

Sister Mary Joseph. Everything I have written about my faith goes back to the ideas and concepts my parish priests taught me as a youngster.

I had the good fortune of being raised during a time when faith was central to family life in this country. Hearing stories of the Blessed Mother from the nuns had a big impact on my life. I have written about faith, family, and the presence of evil in our world. My writings have all been directed toward giving my grandchildren the basics of faith as well as identifying the character traits necessary to lead good lives. If my grandchildren read my words, this effort will be worth it.

Why write a book about the Blessed Virgin for my children and grandchildren? The simple answer is that they probably will not appreciate Mary's virtues and importance to our faith unless I help them along the way. They may go to a Catholic or Christian school, but teachers and even religious leaders may not always give them the "essentials." I am a doubting Thomas in this department.

I firmly believe that parents and grandparents are responsible for instilling a sense of faith in their children and grandchildren. It takes hard work to instill upright character, a sense of charity, discipline, and perseverance in our children. Families that can accomplish this goal give their children a bedrock to build upon to lead productive lives grounded in the truth.

It is only in the later years of my life that I have come to realize the magnificence of the Virgin Mary. I will address some things you may know and even a few things you may not have been exposed to during your faith development, regardless of your religious affiliation. My words have a simple purpose—to share my views and knowledge of our Blessed Mother with others, especially Ayden, Ava, Michael, Sarah, Hunter, Emma, Ryan, and Kate. Like Mom always said to me, "Keep things simple, Michael." I have tried do so in this book.

Hopefully this little book will give everyone a few perspectives on the only human being who never sinned, who answered the call of the angel Gabriel to be the mother of God, and who took on the suffering at the cross as she watched her beloved Son die—Our Blessed Mother. There has never been, nor will there ever be, a mortal being closer to God than the Queen of Heaven and Earth, Mary.

# My Father's Carrier Landings

My father was a fighter pilot in the US Navy for over twenty-five years. He flew missions in the Pacific during World War II and over North Korea during the Korean War. He was highly decorated but never talked about his war medals. He was very humble.

My dad flew his first combat mission at twenty. He had over four thousand flight hours when he retired in 1969. He was raised Catholic and always made sure the family went to church on Sundays. Going to church was a big deal in our family. Church and donuts were the usual routine on Sundays.

In the Navy, a carrier pilot must takeoff and land at sea. The carrier is moving. The plane is moving. There are lots of technical things that must fall into place to safely land "your bird," as Dad would say. There were many casualties in both wars, where the pilot flew his jet into the ocean. Many were saved and some died in freezing-cold temperatures.

My dad was the silent type. When he opened up to me in the later years of his life, he told me about how he calmed his nerves as he made the final approach to his carrier. He said the Hail Mary over and over. He also wore a Miraculous Medal with the Blessed Virgin's image on it.

Dad died at eighty-two from cancer. He died a very painful death. He never took the morphine; he took the pain. He was lucky to have my sister, Joan, at his side to care for him throughout his illness. Joan did the same thing for my mom, who passed in 2002. Her legacy will be the compassionate care she provided both my parents before their deaths.

I saw Dad a week before he died. He was in pain but at peace. He was good with God. I am sure in the last moments of his life, he saw my mother, his mother, and his father. I have no doubt my father is in Heaven. I have no doubt Mary interceded for him and amplified his many prayers to our Lord during my father's lifetime. I believe that the Blessed Mother visited him in the last moments of his life and showed him Heaven's Gate.

# Mothers I Know

Motherhood is the greatest sacrifice a human being can make. A woman gives her body, mind, and soul to her child in order for that life to be nurtured, grow, and become a child of God. This personal sacrifice requires extreme faith and courage. When a woman bears a child, she creates an immortal masterpiece whose soul is eternal. Motherhood is a blessing from the Lord, which requires a lifetime of commitment and dedication.

Before I talk about our Blessed Mother, I would like to talk about three other mothers—my grandmother Anna Sullivan, my mother, Mary Sullivan, and my wife, Dana Sullivan. All these women were and are extraordinary people of great character. Each of them modeled patience, humility, perseverance, and inner strength.

I never met my grandmother, Anna (we called her Annie) Sullivan. She died from a stroke when I was just a child. My father was raised by Annie and her husband, John Patrick Sullivan, during the Great Depression.

Annie was a devout Catholic. She prayed the Rosary every day. She lost her baby boy, Jimmy, when he was five. She raised my dad and his sister, Mary Esther, during very difficult times. My grandfather worked in a shoe factory for fourteen hours a day. He was seldom around because of his hectic work schedule. Annie was a stay-at-home mom. She worked part time washing clothes for her neighbors to make ends meet. She went to daily Mass whenever she could.

My grandmother ensured my dad and his sister were raised with a profound respect for the church and priests. Dad became an altar boy and my aunt helped out in the church.

My dad seldom talked about his mom. When he did, he spoke of her in a very respectful, almost saintly way. He described his mother as humble, loving, and very holy. Dad said she died in bed with a Rosary in her hands.

Annie's impact on my father was profound. Dad was a quiet sufferer. He never complained and always told us kids how lucky we were. He remained silent in Mass and never sang. He was at ease with others and always self-composed. He reflected his mother's character and influence by the way he raised us and led by his example.

My mother, Mary, was also a stay-at-home mom. Her father, William Stiles, was a World War I hero. Grandpa Stiles suffered from depression after the war. Mom lost an older sister, Shirley, when she was three. Her mother, Grace, had to raise the family, as my grandfather worked many long hours in the county courthouse. My grandpa passed away from a stroke when Mom was a senior in high school. I never met my grandfather, but I have a few of his possessions from World War I. He single-handedly charged two German machine gun positions and was awarded a Silver Star for his bravery.

Mom married my dad right after the second world war. When Dad returned from the Pacific, he met my mom in Marlborough, Massachusetts. They married in 1948 and had three children—Joan, Jim, and me. Like his father, my dad was gone a lot from home on naval deployments. When he retired from the navy in 1967, he taught high school business classes for seventeen years.

Mom was always there for us kids. She awoke early, cooked the breakfast, got us off to school, and spent the rest of her day cleaning and taking care of the house. She drove us to all the ball games and devoted her life to motherhood. She never put herself first; it was Dad and the kids that she always unselfishly served. She often told me that all she wanted in life was to be a good wife and mother.

She was not a Catholic, but went to church every Sunday with us. In 1959, she converted to the Catholic faith. I remember her saying to me, "Michael, it just makes sense to me that I should be on the same sheet of music as your father."

Mom was very simplistic in her thinking and in all she did. She made things easy for me to understand and was very patient. She put up with my bad temper and always calmed me down. I could always go to her with my troubles, and her advice was always sound. Mom was very affectionate and always gave me a hug every time we met. I was never too old for a hug from Mom. I looked forward to it.

Mom did without so her children could have the things that she never had growing up. Like Dad, she came from a struggling family that also suffered during the Great Depression.

Mom was hospitalized and in a coma in 2003. Dana, Kerrie, and I rushed down to the hospital to be with her. I held her hand as she passed from this life to the next. I loved my mom and will always be indebted to her for showing me the traits of compassion, loyalty, and unselfishness. If anyone deserved Heaven, Mom certainly did.

My wife, Dana, and I met in 1968 and we have been together ever since. She is intensely honest, and her loyalty to our entire family sets the bar for all of us. She has always been a working mom. She is compassionate, but shows an inner strength that I have seldom seen in others. She is a woman of great character. She is the rock of our family.

Dana will always go the extra mile for our children. She has that rare ability to perfectly balance work and family requirements, but family always comes first with her. As a Marine, like my dad, I spent a lot of time on deployments. Dana ran the household. She was always there for John, Matt, and Kerrie. She never put herself first.

As a registered nurse, she always worked wherever we were stationed. She would do night shifts. After she put the kids to bed, she would catch a couple hours rest before going to work from 11p.m. until 7a.m. Many times, she would do back-to-back shifts on the weekends. Her German blood and "stick-to-it-ness" character always impressed me. I am grateful to God for sending me Dana.

When our son died in 2017, Dana was overwhelmed with grief. She still is, to this day. You never get over the loss of a child. She and John drove to work every day. I have addressed in other writings the effects John's death had on our family. Suffice to say, it was devastating. Dana survived and continues to lead our family with her compassion, drive, and perseverance. She is my girl, now and forever.

The common traits displayed by the mothers I have known are loyalty, patience, humility, and perseverance. These traits mirror those displayed by Our Blessed Mother while here on earth as she raised our Lord, Jesus Christ.

My daughter, Kerrie, and my daughter-in-law, Katy, are also devoted mothers. They keep their families together and sacrifice everything for their children. They get the kids to all the games and are always there to solve all the problems that seem insurmountable for their children. They pick them up when they fall, give them hugs of encouragement, and keep them headed in the right direction. They are continuing in the legacy that their own mothers passed down to them.

Motherhood is the glue that keeps our society together. The strength of mothers and their loyalty to their husbands and children makes this world a better place in which to live. It is through our mothers that we learn how to laugh and when to cry. Mothers teach us to be strong when we feel weak and be compassionate to the less fortunate. They fix us when we are emotionally broken and give us courage to persevere. If we are lucky, our moms bring us closer to God through their examples, which can stay with us for a lifetime.

Motherhood is a blessing from God. All good moms have a special relationship with their children. We should always remember that the first member of the Church was a woman. There will never be a mortal being closer to our Lord than Mary, His mother.

# Faith

In the movie *Forrest Gump,* starring Tom Hanks, there is a scene which has always stayed with me. Forrest is staying with Lieutenant Dan, his wartime army platoon commander, in a run-down New York City hotel room. Lieutenant Dan is in a wheelchair; he lost both legs in Vietnam, but Forrest saved his life. Lieutenant Dan is a bitter, raging alcoholic who is in deep despair. He asks Forrest in a really sarcastic manner, "Have you found Jesus yet. All the guys down at the VFW keep asking me if I have found Jesus." Forrest replies, "I did not know he was lost, Lieutenant Dan." Forrest then says, "I am going to Heaven, Lieutenant Dan." The movie has a great ending; you should watch it!

We never lose the Lord. We move away from Him. We can find Him again, often through his Blessed Mother.

A few months ago, I attended my grandson Hunter's school chapel event. He goes to a Christian school. Hunter's class re-enacted the Bible story where Jesus walks on water. Jesus had delivered his Sermon on the Mount and for the first time prayed the Our Father to the crowd of five thousand.

After turning five loaves of bread and two fish into enough food to feed over five thousand people, he went to a nearby hill to pray. As his apostles were sailing their boat, crossing the Sea of Galilee in the middle of the night, a storm gathered. The apostles saw Jesus walking toward them on the water. They thought Jesus was an apparition and became frightened. Jesus said to Peter, "Come." Peter had faith and exited the boat, walking on water like Jesus. After a few steps, he faltered and fell into the water. Jesus pulled him out and they both returned to the boat. Jesus then calmed the wind and the seas. The apostles now believed Jesus truly was the "Son of God."

If you do not trust in something bigger than yourself and have faith that things can get better, you can easily fall into despair. Like Peter, you will sink. Only God can save you. Hopefully, we all find the Lord in this life. Our faith either moves forward, stalls out, or leaves us. If you are lucky, you will rediscover the importance of God before you pass from this life to the next.

We all have a hard time in trusting each other, let alone God. We want control. We want it our way. Without humility, there can be no faith. We are all powerless to prevent the tragedies and challenges in our life. But we can all learn through our faith to achieve inner peace and true happiness.

There have been tens of thousands of books written about our Blessed Mother. Many saints have had a great devotion to her and thousands of prayers have been written to ask for her intercession. In troubled times when we are facing life's most difficult challenges, we should always turn to Jesus and His Blessed Mother.

Character and faith are interwoven. Helping others, sacrificing for your family, setting the example, being honest and forthright; these are all traits we can learn from our Blessed Mother. She is a model of virtue, purity, and humility for all of us. She is the Earthly Mother of our Lord and the Queen of Heaven. No mortal being was ever closer to Jesus than His mother.

You cannot discuss the life and spiritual intercessory powers of our Blessed Mother in isolation of our Lord. Jesus and Mary are inextricably linked in Holy Scripture. Our Lord's reign is supreme and His mother's Immaculate Heart is a beacon of light for all of us to come and worship her merciful Son.

# A Well-Formed Conscience

As Christians, we believe that we are obligated to faithfully follow what we know to be right and just. Sounds simple enough. But if you are not grounded in truth and faith, you may not be able to distinguish good from evil. This is especially difficult in a world where moral boundaries seem blurred. We all need reference points to guide us through the difficulties of life.

When I was growing up, the term "Does your conscience bother you" was used by my mom and dad after I had done something out of line. I do not hear this term used too much today.

So, what does your conscience have to do with Jesus and His Blessed Mother? In a word, everything. If we never develop a moral code to live by, we can lose our way and get lost in a very secular world. Distractions and meaningless goals will take over our lives. Without a well-formed conscience, you may never develop an interior life focused on faith.

As a child, my father taught me to tell the truth "no matter how bad it hurt." My mom taught me to "never make fun of other people." My grandfather taught me the value of working hard and to never quit. I can still hear his words, "Michael, a job worth doing is worth doing well." Perhaps the greatest advice I ever got was from my dad: "Think for yourself, son."

My parents, along with my teachers and the church, gave me a solid grounding on what was acceptable behavior and what was not. I had a moral code to live by. If I stepped over the line, a little voice in my head would ring out "stop," to let me know I was doing something wrong.

I felt bad when I told a lie or cheated on a test. I was not perfect and had lots of run-ins with sin. But I got through some tough years, with what I believe to be a well-formed conscience. Oh, one other thing; I always wanted to make my parents proud of me. I did not want to disappoint them and wanted to live up to their expectations. And all my teachers moved me in a positive direction.

Unlike the years I grew up, there is now an internet, a very secular world, and an unlimited range of choices. Kids are bombarded with feelings, not necessarily facts. School is supposed to be about the three "Rs"—reading, 'riting, and 'rithmetic (it was spelled wrong to make it rhyme). Raising kids is a very difficult job for all parents. You have to work overtime to give your children a Christian perspective and to develop a love of God.

Christians have a serious and lifelong obligation to form their consciences and those of their children. Conscience is not something that allows us to justify doing whatever we want, nor is it a mere "feeling" about what we should or should not do. The truth is that our conscience is the voice of God resounding in our heart, revealing the truth to us and calling us to do what is good. A well-formed conscience helps us to avoid evil and make sound moral judgments.

A well-formed conscience allows you to embrace goodness and truth.

I hope my grandchildren will develop a profound respect for our Blessed Mother and her special relationship with her Son. If they live their lives with faith and purpose, it is because they have developed a well-formed conscience.

By listening to our parents, praying, studying the Bible, and our church teachings, we begin to achieve wisdom, which will guide our decision-making. Once we achieve interior peace through reflection and prayer, it is easier for the Lord and His Mother to communicate with us. We begin to realize that we are not alone, and there is always help if we knock on that door.

# The Presence of Evil

We are always at an "inflection point" in history. There are events in our world that can alter our lives and the future of the planet. People can view inflection points as either positive or negative. Some recent examples of inflection points include the end to the Cold War, the innovations of the internet, and the recent attacks on the family and the right to life.

Many people have turned a blind eye toward evil and suffering. In a word, some have become "oblivious" to events that are tearing our faith and families apart. There are things worth fighting for and dying for in this life. If there is no order, there is disorder.

The definition of life has become blurred in our society. Words like "pro-choice" seem to indicate a democratic ideal. In reality, they support the killing of innocent children in a mother's womb.

"Wokeness" is today's new word for disorder. Teaching children that they can be either sex is against the laws of nature. Teaching young people that this country is systemically racist is simply a lie. If you don't understand the facts laid out in history and view them contextually in the times they occurred, you wind up with critical race theory and racial disharmony. If we did a better job in public schools of teaching history instead of trashing it, we would give our kids a better grasp of the facts. Facts, not feelings or narratives, reveal this country was built on four words, "In God We Trust." We are in troubled times. We all need to look toward God and Holy Scripture to get us out of this mess we got ourselves into.

We are in a war. "Diabolical disorientation has been hurled over the world," as predicted by Saint John Paul II. The issues of abortion, gender identification, crime, drug abuse, divorce, attack on the nuclear family, corrupt leadership, and social discord are all the Devil's work. The Church is under attack, but we know the outcome; God wins. We are either with the winning side, or not. It is that simple. Don't complicate it!

One of my favorite spiritual leaders of the 20th century was Bishop Fulton Sheen. Check out his 1950s and 1960s videos on YouTube. Bishop Sheen's television shows cover a wide variety of topics, including faith, fear, selfishness, sin, and the Devil, to name a few. Everything he talks about is relevant in today's world. He talks about the evils of communism, out-of-control crime, drug abuse, abortion on demand; sound familiar? Here is what he says about the Devil:

"Do not mock the Gospels and say there is no Satan. Evil is too real in the world to say that. Do not say that Satan is dead and gone. Satan never gathers so many cohorts as when in his shrewdness, he spreads the rumor of his death. Do not reject the Gospel when it says that Jesus was tempted by the Devil. Satan always temps the pure; the others are already his."

Today it is very clear that the Devil is attacking two primary targets: our faith and our families. The Devil seeks to create doubt, confusion, and anxiety in our lives. He wants us focused only on our own needs, at the expense of others. He loves to present us with distractions. Addiction, depression, selfishness, anger, and pride are his chief allies.

The God of the Old Testament is a just God, but he leveled many civilizations and cities that failed to heed his Word and disobeyed Him. The God of the New Testament, Jesus Christ, is a merciful Savior. But look closely at the Gospels. He came as a divider and not as a unifier. There are many passages that refer to separating the wheat from the chaff and the "wailing and gnashing of teeth" for those who fail to heed his words.

If you do not believe that evil exists, you will not attempt to amend your life and get closer to God. The more comfortable you become with sinning, the easier it is to just say, "Why pray? What is going to happen is going to happen, and there is nothing we can do about it." That is like saying, why practice or why study? We need to move forward in our lives, especially in our spiritual lives.

We should not be defined by others, and we should never give up on becoming the best version of ourselves. Progress is what we are looking for in life. None of us are perfect but that does not mean we should not strive for perfection physically, mentally, and spiritually. We all have a yardstick to live by and to measure our progress—Jesus Christ.

We will all experience what some saints have referred to as "the dark night of the soul." We lose hope. We feel that God has deserted us or that He does not love us. We feel abandoned. This is not God moving away from us. This is the

Devil at work to tear down our faith and capture our soul. God gives us free will, to either wallow in self-pity or slowly work our way back into the light. It is our choice.

During our deployment to Somalia in 1992, our Marine Corps Task Force had a Catholic chaplain, Father Sodano. Every Sunday he would get on a helicopter and ride over one-hundred miles to say Mass at our command post in Bardera. We normally had about one-hundred Marines attend Mass. "There are no atheists in foxholes, Michael." My father's words rang true throughout my career in the Marines. We were in a lot of desperate situations over the years, but our chaplains were always there to give us spiritual direction and guidance. No matter what their faith, Catholic, Protestant or Jewish, each was selfless and devoted to saving souls.

In one sermon, Father Sodano talked about the tapestry God weaves for each of us. I remember him saying:

We look up and see this tapestry from our vantage point on Earth. The tapestry cloth looks frayed at times. There are gaps and holes that need to be filled in order to complete it. But the other view of this tapestry is from the top-down, the Lord's perspective. He wants to make our tapestry perfect and beautiful to behold. He wants it to be a tapestry of hope, joy, and one that is in total harmony with his Word. He wants all of us to be perfected, so that he can show us the many mansions he has provided for us in Heaven. You may think your life is coming apart and breaking. But with God at your side, your life will be amended, and in the end the tapestry will be completed. It will be perfect and magnificent to behold. We just need to trust in God's love for each of us.

Our job in completing our tapestry is to listen, pray, and trust that, when we draw our last breath, our tapestry will be acceptable to God. It is that simple. If the tapestry remains incomplete, it is because we have failed to comply with the will of God. Instead of listening, we convince ourselves that our way is the best path. We deny the inevitable, which is death, and focus only on the secular aspects of life. We become lost. We become resentful, and we become selfish. We fail to see the goodness in our fellow man and want only power and earthly rewards. This is a recipe for spiritual disaster. Our ship will take on too much water and it will sink!

Prayer is the most powerful weapon we have to achieve happiness and deal with evil. It is what we need in our everyday lives to stay close to God. If we accept the fact that we are made in the image of our Heavenly Father, we realize the need to stay in touch with Him in good times and when things go wrong.

So we should pray unceasingly for guidance from the Lord. We should be grateful for the gifts he has bestowed upon us. Above all, we must be courageous and stand up for our beliefs, especially today.

God wants us to succeed, but our obedience is required to get through the narrow door referred to in the New Testament. Life is not meant to be a series of wins with no losses. We all fail. God measures our faith by our obedience to his Word, not by our successes. Remember, some of the first will be last and some of the last will be first. We are judged not on what we accomplish in this life but rather how we focus and direct our efforts toward the next life with God.

So how do we defeat the Devil and move closer to Jesus? We have lots of weapons in our arsenal: prayer, our church fellowship, reading passages from the Bible, etc. The list of friendly allies we have in our fight is endless. We need to do battle and not sit on the sidelines. The stakes are high.

God gives us many tools to overcome evil. I have said the Hail Mary many times. Sister Mary Joseph always said, "Mary is Jesus's mother, children, and she was the only perfect human being ever born." That was simple enough for me in second grade. I still believe it to this day.

If we lose our soul to the Devil, we will spend eternity in darkness—scares me! Just like the nuns taught us in elementary school, "You need to talk to God every day, Michael, and ask Him for help with the big and little problems in your life. He will always be there for you."

# Crushing the Head of the Serpent

"The two means for saving the world are prayer and sacrifice. There is no problem, I tell you, no matter how difficult it is, that we cannot resolve by the prayer of the Holy Rosary. With the Holy Rosary we will sanctify ourselves. We will console Our Lord and obtain the salvation of many souls. Finally, devotion to the Immaculate Heart of Mary, our most holy Mother, consists in considering Her as the seat of mercy, of goodness and of pardon, and as the sure door of entering Heaven." —Sister Lùcia, 1957

The above quote by sister Lùcia, one of the three children who were visited by Our Blessed Mother in 1917 at Fatima, Portugal, says it all. Prayer is the key to solving all the problems in our world today and tomorrow. If you are a Christian, you may know about the story of Our Lady of Fatima. The three secrets of Fatima provided by our Blessed Mother are the key to understanding what is happening to our world today, as well as what we need to do to avoid the destruction of our world.

There is a statue of Mary crushing the head of a serpent that depicts the final victory of good over evil. The powers of darkness will be destroyed through our prayers. Prayer leads to the grace God gives each of us to persevere and overcome all that life throws at us.

Mary is beauty, grace, and humility. The Hail Mary is both prophetic and a source of great hope to all of us:

***Hail Mary, full of grace, the lord is with thee. Blessed art thou amongst women, and blessed is the fruit of thy womb, Jesus. Holy Mary, Mother of God, pray for us sinners now and at the hour of our death. Amen.***

The greatest friendly force working to help us fight and defeat the Evil One is our Blessed Mother. Of all the human beings that have been born and will ever be born, only Mary was born without the stain of original sin on her soul.

Mary's family lived in Nazareth. Her parents, Joachim and Anne, are thought to have suffered from infertility. As they grew older, they worried that they would never be able to conceive. Tradition says that an angel appeared to Joachim and Anne and promised that they would have a child. That child was Mary.

So what do Catholics believe about Mary? It is all in the Apostles Creed, including the proclamation that our Lord was "conceived by the power of the Holy Spirit and born of the Virgin Mary." If we accept the fact that God needed a perfect vessel to introduce His Son into the world, and the fact that Mary raised and was with Jesus until he was thirty years of age, we can begin to appreciate the importance God places in her. Of the billions of women who have been born and will be born, God chose Mary to be the mother of Jesus.

Many people cannot understand why Catholics pray to Mary. Some say it is sacrilegious to pray to anyone other than God. They have it wrong. We don't pray to Mary; we pray for her intercession. Mary opens the door to Jesus, and Jesus opens the door to the Father. Our Blessed Mother is the shortest route to Jesus.

When I was in the Marines, I commanded several units from platoon through battalion level. At each command level, you have the commander and an executive officer we call the XO. The XO's job is to assist the commander and serve as a filter for all issues within the command. Whether it is a personnel problem, a logistics problem, or an operational problem, the XO can usually solve the problem and coordinate a resolution to promote efficiency and morale within the unit. The XO can advise the commander, but only the commander can make a final decision. The XO is the most trusted asset to the commander.

Mary is like our XO. She is the Queen of Heaven and always has the ear of her beloved Son. I am not suggesting that we should only talk to Mary and avoid praying to God, our Father. Our relationship with the Lord should be deeply personal. I am saying that our Blessed Mother can intercede for us and amplify our prayers to make them extremely powerful. Remember Cana? Jesus performed a miracle because his mother asked Him to do so.

Mary is not Divine in nature as the Father, Son, and the Holy Spirit are in the Holy Trinity. She is, however, the most powerful intercessor in Heaven who can protect us from the Devil and his influence over us. She is human perfection and has been given special intercessor powers from our Lord to help all of us in our moments of doubt and despair. The Devil fears her! As the Queen of Heaven, she rules over all the saints and angels.

Mary was young, poor, and female. These qualities made her unsuitable to be close to God in the eyes of many

Jewish people. But God saw Mary's qualities of trust and obedience. He knew she would willingly serve Him in the most important calling ever given to a human being. God knew that Mary was a woman of rare strength. Mary was willing to submit her entire life to God's plan, no matter what it cost her.

I saw many great leadership examples in the Marines. We were forced to memorize fourteen leadership traits and eleven leadership principles. These principles and traits provided a blueprint for leading young men and women. Our Blessed Mother modeled every one of these. She was patient, compassionate, honest, decisive, responsible, dependable—the list is endless. Her life reflects sacrifice, devotion to the Holy Family, and unsurpassed faith in our Lord. She had to accept the challenge of being the mother of God's Son, knowing that someday He would be taken away from her. I do not think she could have imagined the pain of her Son's death. I do think that she knew her life would be filled with sacrifice.

Let's clear up the misconception that Mary was an unwed mother. She was not. Catholics believe that Mary was betrothed and legally married to her husband, Joseph, when the angel Gabriel asked her to be the mother of our Lord (The Annunciation). During the first century, Jewish weddings had two stages. Husbands had a short time, upwards of a year, after the wedding to prepare a home for their new wife. After this first stage, the husband and wife lived together and the marriage could only be broken by death or divorce. By bringing his wife into the home and beginning married life together, the marriage process was completed according to Jewish Law. Mary was not living with Joseph when the Annunciation took place, but they were legally married.

Once Mary was told by the Angel Gabriel that she was with child, she said, "How can this be, since I have no relations with a man" (Luke 1:26-38). Mary probably thought Joseph would divorce her. She may have even thought about death by stoning, which was the Jewish law if a woman became pregnant out of wedlock or committed adultery. Thank God the Blessed Mother said, " Behold I am the handmaid of the Lord. May it be done to me according to your word." (Luke 1:26-38)

This prayer from Saint Louis de Montfort sums up what our relationship should be with the Virgin Mary:

Mary is the fruitful virgin, and in all the souls in which she comes to dwell she causes to flourish purity of heart and body, rightness of intention and abundance of good works. Do not imagine that Mary, the most faithful of creatures who gave birth to God, remains barren in the faithful soul. It will be she who makes the soul live incessantly for Jesus Christ, and will make Jesus live in the soul.

When I was sixteen, I got in "over my head" surfing in the Pacific Ocean. I had been surfing only a few months. My friends talked me into paddling out to catch waves in some big surf. The waves were breaking about a half mile offshore and easily measured fifteen feet. Back in those days there were no leashes and if you lost your board, you swam to shore. My mind kept telling me not to paddle out, but my pride took over and I entered the water.

I finally made it to where the waves were breaking, and a huge wave smashed me down. I lost my board, as did all the other guys out there. A fog bank was starting to come in, and I lost sight of my friends. I had to swim to shore in some strong current. Fog, current, no surfboard; it was the most dangerous situation I had ever been in.

I did the best I could to calm myself down, but I kept thinking, "I don't want to die out here. I want to see my family again." I used the breaststroke, which I learned as a youngster, to slowly make my way to shore. I started saying the Hail Mary repeatedly. It took me forty-five minutes to make it to shore, and I came in about a mile north of where I had entered the water. I believe to this day that those Hail Mary's turned the tide for me and got me safely to shore.

Fear grips all of us at some time or another in our lives. Everybody is afraid of something. Fear is part of life. Extreme fear can bring on the "flight or fight" syndrome. You must conquer your fears in life. If you don't, you will probably never reach your goals and expectations. When you conquer your fears, you grow.

Fear of dying is natural. Most of us don't think about our last day on Earth. That said, it is always good to remind ourselves that only the rocks live forever. Take a daily inventory of where you are in your faith. Living in friendship with the Lord is the only way to fight through your earthly fears and focus on what is important—your salvation.

I learned the Hail Mary from Sister Mary Joseph when I was in second grade. I have said it often during my life. I said it before an important test in school, before a big game in sports, before I went to bed at night, and sometimes after I lost a friend. I said the words, but did not fully understand their meaning until later in life.

Mary is full of "grace." I always had a hard time understanding this word growing up. Grace is interior peace and accepting the Lord's undeserved help in all we do. God filled Mary with grace from the moment of her Immaculate Conception; another hard term I had to wrestle with as a child. I learned later in life that unlike us, the Blessed Virgin was born without any original sin. What is original sin?

Adam and Eve trusted in God. They obeyed his commandments. But they lost faith, let their pride get the better of them, and disobeyed God. Their fall from grace resulted in all the problems we now experience as humans—fear, sickness, famine, war, depression, sin, etc. All of us are born in a state of original sin because of our first parents' fall. Only Mary was born without original sin. We all need baptism to be able to fully accept God's grace and remove original sin from our souls.

Even baptism is a hard concept for many to understand. Why do we have infants baptized? Why don't we wait until they can fully comprehend the Lord and accept him into their hearts? There are varying opinions on these issues. My only comment here is that I am glad I was baptized as an infant. The Christian faith has one goal: keeping us in friendship with our Savior. The earlier we remove original sin from our souls, the easier it is to find our Lord.

# Church Teachings on Mary

The four Catholic undisputed teachings (dogmas) on our Blessed Mother are: Mary is the Mother of God, Mary is the Perpetual Virgin, Mary's birth was an Immaculate Conception, and Mary's Body and Soul were assumed into Heaven.

In addition to attending mass every Sunday, Catholics have five holy days of obligation during the year where mass attendance is required. Two of these five are in celebration of our Blessed Mother; Mary the Mother of God, on January 1st of each year and the Assumption of Mary, celebrated on August 15th.

A few years ago, one of our church leaders asked me if I would do the readings at Monday's 6p.m. Mass. This past Monday was the Assumption of Mary celebration, and I had the opportunity to read the following passage from Saint John's Book of Revelation:

"And a great portent appeared in Heaven, a woman clothed with the sun, with the moon under her feet, and on her head a crown of twelve stars; she was with child and she cried out in her pangs of birth, in anguish for delivery. And another portent appeared in Heaven; behold, a great red dragon, with seven heads and ten horns, and seven diadems upon his heads. His tail swept down a third of the stars of Heaven, and cast them to the earth. And the dragon stood before the woman who was about to bear a child, that he might devour her child when she brought it forth; she brought forth a male child, one who is to rule all the nations with a rod of iron, but her child was caught up to God and to his throne, and the woman fled into the wilderness, where she has a place prepared by God, in which to be nourished for one thousand two hundred and sixty days."

There has been much debate over who or what the woman symbolizes. The Church, Israel, or the Virgin Mother have all been identified as "the woman clothed in the sun." There is no doubt in my mind that the woman is our Blessed Mother. The dragon is the Devil, who seeks to devour the child (Jesus) and his followers.

Jesus was conceived by the Holy Spirit. Catholics call this the Incarnation. The Holy Spirit came upon Mary and placed our Lord in her womb. She did not have relations with a man at any time during her life. She had no other children. She is the Perpetual Virgin. Faith is trust. I trust this church teaching.

Many Protestants believe Mary had other children. They site passages in the Bible to support their argument that, for example, James was a brother to Jesus. I am not going to try to solve any of these issues here in this little book.

I will point out that at the foot of the cross, a dying Jesus said to His apostle John, "Son, behold your Mother." Jesus then said to Mary, "Mother, behold your Son." After the crucifixion and resurrection of Jesus, Mary lived with Saint John in Ephesus, which is in modern day Turkey. So, if Jesus had brothers and sisters, why did Mary live with John and not her other children? The answer to me is simple: Jesus had no siblings. Once again, I trust the church teaching on this issue.

Early church tradition was that Joseph was a widower who married the Virgin Mary later in life, after he already had a family with his first wife. A later tradition holds that he was a virgin himself and that the brothers of Jesus were other relatives, perhaps cousins. Because we simply don't know, Catholics are free to believe either tradition. All that is required is to believe that Mary remained a perpetual virgin, including throughout her marriage to Joseph. I also trust in this Catholic teaching.

We ask Mary to pray for us. Jesus made her the Queen of Heaven and the Mother of the Church. One might ask, What church?

Today there are thousands of Christian churches and hundreds of denominations. We have different religions as well. But the church founded by Jesus Christ was the universal or Catholic church. For Catholics, Matthew 16:18 is a key passage when establishing a biblical basis for the papacy (Pope) and the establishment of the church: "And I tell you, you are Peter, and on this rock, I will build my church, and the powers of death shall not prevail against it."

Before I go any farther, let me address the "big white elephant in the room." A lot of people say that it does not matter what church you belong to, as long as you accept Jesus. I agree that accepting Jesus as our Savior is absolutely essential to salvation.

"Once saved, always saved" may or may not be true. I'm used to a life where I have to work for things to get ahead. Mom and Dad always told me if I worked hard, I could attain anything in this life. Your work ethic is extremely important, no matter what your pursuits are in life. It was for me in and out of the Marines. So, to me nothing in life comes easy. You must suffer through all the trials and challenges and persevere to accomplish your goals.

Your spiritual life needs to be reflected in all aspects of your interactions with others. Being a "man of God" was a compliment in the nineteenth century. Today, I'm not so sure. Our secular society is trying to cancel God. Closing churches during a pandemic and keeping bars open is an indication that a society, once God-fearing, may be on life support.

There is a lot of Bible interpretation that has gone on in our world. Remember, the birth of Protestantism was the result, to a large extent, of Martin Luther's interpretation of the Bible. He had disagreements with the Catholic Church's leadership, but it was his interpretation of the Word that led to the Lutheran Church being founded. Remember, Luther was a Catholic priest.

Saint Paul says faith without good works is empty faith. He writes: "For he [God] will render to every man according to his works." We need to put our faith into action by reaching out to others and being Good Samaritans. I firmly believe the way you live your life, and the charity you show to others matter in the mercy God will grant us in the end.

Your church may have its own interpretation of the Bible, and that's fine. Catholics believe that because Jesus made Peter the first pope, his papal successors remain head of the Christian Church here on Earth. You can disagree with which church or denomination has it right. It is hard to disagree that the Catholic Church was the one founded by Christ. It is in the Bible!

# Jesus and His Mother

Mary is prophesized in the Old Testament. She appears by name in the gospels of Matthew, Mark, Luke, and John as well as Acts of the Apostles. Luke contains the most references to Mary and places the greatest emphasis on her role in God's plan. Mary is mentioned by name in the genealogy of Jesus, in the Annunciation, in Mary's visit with Elizabeth, in the birth of Jesus, in the visit of the wise men, and throughout the New Testament. Mary knew about the Old Testament prophesizing the coming of a Messiah. What she did not know was that she was going to be the Messiah's mother.

We could write volumes about the relationship between Jesus and his mother. We could cite historical facts, Bible passages, church teachings, and theologian's interpretations. I will not do that. However, one cannot discuss the Blessed Mother without discussing the works and teachings of her Son. The "Divine" interfaces with the "perfect" in their relationship. Mary was the perfect vessel to deliver her Divine Son to our world.

Mary is the new Eve. I never really understood this concept and relationship until the later years of my life. Today, I understand that God created Adam and Eve to be perfect creatures and wanted them to live in paradise. Both enjoyed a direct and perfect relationship with the Father, God. There was no sin in the world until Eve ate from the Tree of

Knowledge and Adam followed her lead. We all know what resulted—a sinful world of temptation and misery. But it is a world of choices, where we can use our free will to move closer to God. The Father will always love us. It is we who must embrace His love, through our love for ourselves and others.

Free will means we have to suffer. Our flesh is prone to sin. However, our souls can move closer to God and overcome our inclination to sin. Each day we have a battle raging in our soul between good and evil. It is like a tug-of-war, which side wins is up to us. We fight back against our sinful impulses through prayer and our faith that God will save us from damnation. Simple enough in theory, but we all know how hard it is not to sin.

We need to think as children when it comes to our faith. Christ loved the "little ones." I always reflect on my second-grade teacher's advice. Sister Mary Joseph had it right. What she told me in second grade about my faith has stood the test of time. She was a simple Irish nun who gave all her students a simple view of life. She identified for us our responsibilities to our family and to our church in ways we eight-year-olds could all understand.

As adults our thirst for knowledge is a two-edged sword. As we acquire information, we can use it to bolster our belief system and understanding of life. We can achieve wisdom through the acquisition of knowledge and real-world experiences.

In contrast, many people use information as the means to challenge ideas and support their position on an issue.

This can be very useful in many aspects of our lives. Being educated in history, medical science, philosophy, or any other academic field can be the means to identify our vocations and achieve success in our future pursuits.

We need to always look at both sides of an issue. If we cannot at least appreciate our opponent's point of view, we are in danger of defaulting to the "I'm right, you are wrong, position." This is a recipe for disaster in this life.

As we become more exposed to complex matters surrounding our faith and the other issues in our world, our critical thinking skills become extremely important. We need to think things through and arrive at our own conclusions. We should always refine our knowledge and seek to grow mentally, physically, and spiritually in this life. Through knowledge and experience, we gain wisdom.

We need to understand that our "thinking" enables us to steer our lives in a positive direction. This is where our church doctrine becomes important. One thing I have learned in life is that there are rarely any original ideas put forth concerning the Christian faith. Everything laid out in the Bible is applicable to today's world. There truly is "nothing new under the sun."

The problem comes when we put too much information into our heads. We listen to too many views on a subject. We question everything. We complicate simple truths with too many questions. Is the world really round? Is there really a universe outside of this one? Is there really a Heaven or a Hell? Was Jesus really God? I think you get my drift.

We "overthink" and become confused. We can become so hardened that we question everything and believe in nothing. I know so many people today who are completely turned off by religion. Sad. Especially when you think about what is at risk—our immortal souls.

In Catholic school, we studied Bible passages every week. I remember being confused about words like annunciation, assumption, passion, sacrifice, Holy Spirit, Trinity, etc. But sister Mary Joseph always made things seem easy for me and my classmates to understand. She often said things like, "Don't worry about the word, just know that it is a good thing and a gift from God."

Sister Mary Joseph had a lasting impression on my faith, as did all my teachers at Blessed Sacrament School. It was in her classroom that I first learned about the Apostles, the Nativity, the Holy Family's flight to Egypt, Jesus's teaching in the Temple, the Good Samaritan gospel, and the Crucifixion. I cannot remember her exact words on any of these subjects. I do remember the impressions the stories had on me. Most of her talks took place around religious holidays, like Christmas and Easter. Let me try to capture the essence of those impressions. As best as I recall, Sister Mary said (I paraphrase of course):

*"Mary was very poor. She was young, probably in her teens. An angel visited her and told her not to be afraid. The angel said she was going to be the mother of God. Mary was really scared because she was a virgin. Sister Mary said this event was called the Annunciation. At the age of eight, I just accepted Sister Mary Joseph's words as completely true, and I still do.*

*Sister Mary said, Joseph was also visited by an angel who told him not to be afraid and to stay married to Mary. Jesus was born in a stable in Bethlehem because there was no room for him in the local inn. Many shepherds and the Three Wiseman visited the baby Jesus."*

*Mary and Joseph were both Jews. They followed all the Jewish laws and traditions. When the baby was eight days old, he was given the name Jesus. When Jesus was about one month old, his parents took him to Jerusalem to be presented at the Temple. At that time, a man named Simeon lived in Jerusalem. Simeon was a very respected religious leader. The Holy Spirit allowed Simeon to recognize Jesus as the Messiah. But Simeon predicted the Crucifixion and the great sorrow it would bring to Mary.*

*King Herod wanted to kill the baby Jesus because he was afraid Jesus would be more powerful than him. Herod was very cruel and evil and ordered all the little boys under two years of age around Bethlehem killed. Once again, an angel visited Joseph and told him to take Jesus and Mary to the country of Egypt to escape from Herod.*

*The Holy family traveled to Egypt and spent a few years there before another angel told Joseph it was safe to return to the town of Nazareth. Joseph was a carpenter, and he worked every day alongside Jesus. Mary took care of all the household chores. They were a very happy family. Joseph was very protective and very humble.*

*When Jesus was twelve, the Holy Family traveled to Jerusalem to visit the Temple. When they returned, Mary and Joseph thought Jesus was with some other families. But soon they discovered Jesus was not with anyone in their group. Mary and Joseph were very worried and returned to Jerusalem. They found Jesus at the Temple with the other Jewish leaders. Jesus asked questions, and everyone realized just how smart He was about religious matters. When Mary saw Jesus, she starting crying and asked Jesus why He had not told them where He was going. Jesus said that Mary and Joseph should have known that He had to be in his "Father's house doing his Father's work."*

The next thing that Sister Mary Joseph told us about was the wedding at Cana, when Jesus performed his first miracle by changing water into wine. Just before Easter vacation (yes, we called it Easter vacation, not spring break, in the 1950s) she talked about John the Baptist. Here is what I remember from her little talks:

*Our Blessed Mother had a cousin who was named Elizabeth. Elizabeth also had a baby she called John. John grew up and spent all his time in the desert praying and telling people to change their evil ways because the Messiah was coming. He told people to repent (another word I had a hard time understanding).*

*When Jesus was about thirty, he went to the Jordan River and met John. John was baptizing people, and Jesus asked John to baptize him. John knew that Jesus was God, but Jesus wanted John to baptize him. When John placed Jesus in the water, a white dove flew over Jesus and a voice from Heaven cried out, "This is my Son, in whom I am well pleased."*

Sister Mary Joseph also told us about the apostles and all the miracles Jesus performed. She talked about Jesus's powers to heal the blind, the crippled, and people who were crazy. I was only eight, so crazy meant to me someone who yelled and screamed. Crazy was someone you put in a hospital. The lady down the street from where we lived got crazy and cut off all her hair. She had kids and they all went away when their mom was hospitalized. This is what happened to crazy people in the 1950s. When Sister Mary Joseph told me Jesus cured the crazy, I was really impressed.

Sister Mary Joseph spent a good amount of time talking about angels. She told us that we all had a guardian angel who would help us to fight the Devil and protect us from danger. Her face always smiled when she talked about the angels, especially Saint Michael. She read a book to us about how Saint Michael defeated the Devil and kicked him out of Heaven and into Hell. I was really impressed with the way she told this story. I wanted to be like Saint Michael, especially since my name was Michael.

Just before Easter, she also talked about Good Friday. I had a hard time calling the death of Jesus on the cross a "good" thing. Later in life, I figured it out. Sister Mary said, "Jesus died on the cross so our sins could all be forgiven. On Easter Sunday Jesus arose from the dead and visited his Mother and all of his apostles. After forty days, Jesus went back into Heaven to be with His Father. He will come again and all good people will join Him in Heaven. If you want to get to Heaven, you must love Jesus, say your prayers, and always be kind to others."

That is what sticks out in my mind from second grade. It has been sixty-five years since I listened to Sister Mary Joseph's little talks. She is long gone from this Earth, but I am sure she is in Heaven. Next to mom and dad, she was the biggest influence on my childhood faith development.

# Seven Sorrows

We often forget how much Our Lady suffered during her life. Her greatest period of suffering occurred as she had to watch her Son die on his cross. Another title for the Virgin Mary is our "Lady of Sorrows."

I have talked a little in my previous books about the death of my beautiful son, John. He was married and had two great kids, Ava and Ayden. He fell into despair and took his life at forty years of age. I think about my boy every hour of every day. My family suffered a crushing loss. But our Blessed Mother suffered more than any of us will ever experience in this life. On a lonely hill outside of Jerusalem, she had to endure untold suffering as she watched the lifeblood of her Son drain out from his disfigured, torn body.

Mary is the New Eve. Unlike the original Eve, she never strayed from God and His Commandments. She never listened to the "Evil One." She never let her pride affect her decision-making and always did what followed our Lord's wishes. When she did ask for something, it was on behalf of others and not herself, as she did at Cana for the wedding couple.

Catholics recognize seven events in Mary's life that caused her untold sorrow. Three of them we have already talked about—The prophesy of Simeon that a sword would pierce her heart, the flight into Egypt with the Holy Family to protect the baby Jesus, and losing Jesus for three days until Mary and Joseph found Him at the Temple in Jerusalem.

If someone has ever told you that you will suffer great pain for your child, you may appreciate how Mary felt as Simeon told her that her child was destined to be the rise and fall of many in Jerusalem and that a sword would pierce her heart. If you have ever lost a child while shopping in a grocery store or at a Walmart, you may know the feeling of absolute despair and fear that can overcome a parent until you find your little boy or girl. If you have ever had to leave behind all you own in the middle of the night and travel to a place you know nothing about, it may help you appreciate what the flight to Egypt was like for the Holy Family.

The remaining four sorrows all relate to the crucifixion of our Lord. These sorrows are: Mary meeting Jesus while He was carrying his cross on the way to Calvary, the Crucifixion and death of Jesus, the body of Jesus being taken down from the cross, and the burial of Jesus in the tomb.

The Mel Gibson film, *The Passion of the Christ* vividly portrays the horrors of Jesus's crucifixion. All Christian churches today have simple crosses to symbolize Jesus's supreme sacrifice for all of us. Catholic churches, however, always have an image of Jesus hanging from his cross. For all of us, recognizing the suffering our Lord endured on the last day of his earthly life is redemptive. If you watch *The Passion of the Christ*, you will see the body of Christ in a horrified condition. Roman crucifixion was the cruelest of deaths during the first century. Was the crucifixion really that bad?

Saint Anne Catherine Emmerich was an Augustinian nun who lived from 1774 until 1824. The Catholic church describes her as a "Marian Visionary and Stigmatist." She was canonized (made a saint) in 2004 by Saint John Paul II. While she was alive, she suffered the wounds of Christ on her hands and feet. We call this the "Stigmata." She also had various visions throughout her life. Her visions were recorded in two books authored by Clemens Brentano in the 1840s.

Saint Anne Catherine's visions referenced the exact details of Jesus's Passion, including His suffering in the Garden of Gethsemane on the eve of His crucifixion, His trial in front of Pontius Pilate, His scourging (beating) at the pillar, His carrying of His cross to Calvary, His meeting with His mother Mary on His way to Calvary, His nailing to the cross, His death, Mary holding His body after being taken down from the cross, and His burial in the tomb. All these events are recorded in the *Dolorous Passion of the Christ.* You can read it on the internet. It is quite powerful and very detailed. This is the document Mel Gibson used to make *The Passion of the Christ.* So when you watch the film, and all Christians should at some time, remember the horror you see was revealed to a simple nun by the Holy Spirit.

The feast of our Lady of Sorrows dates back to the 12th century. The image of Our Lady of Sorrows shows Mary with seven swords piercing her heart. The swords represent her painful sorrows. Along with Mary's great sorrow came great love—love of her family, love for the God of the Old Testament, but most especially her love for her Son, our Lord.

Mary sacrificed her entire life for Jesus. She never complained on the journey to Egypt. She never backed away from the suffering that Simeon prophesized. She endured incredible worry before she found her twelve-year-old Son in the Temple. She looked into the eyes of her Son as He fell from the weight of His cross on the way to calvary. Mary never left His side at the foot of the cross, as our Lord endured the cruelest punishment known to man. She held His body after He was taken down from His cross. Finally, she cleaned the broken and bloody body of our Lord and placed Him in a tomb. Love is what Mary exhibited throughout her life. Unparalleled love. That is why Jesus made her the Mother of His Church.

Saint Anne also had visions of the Virgin Mary's life after Jesus was resurrected. Mary traveled to Ephesus and lived with Saint John for twelve years. She visited Jerusalem twice during this period, according to Saint Anne's visions.

The Apostle John is said to have built a house for Mary. The house was built just outside the city, overlooking the ocean and several islands. Unlike many of the other houses in the Christian community, John used rock to construct the house. According to the visions of Saint Anne Catherine, Mary died at age sixty-four and her body and soul were assumed into Heaven. We call this the Assumption of Mary, and it is celebrated as a holy day in the Catholic Church. Mary sits at her Son's right hand as Queen of Heaven and Earth. The foundation for the teaching is rooted in Scripture, specifically in John's mysterious and apocalyptic vision recorded in Revelation 12.

Based on her descriptions of where the house was located outside of Ephesus, a French priest found the structure in 1881. The Catholic Church has taken no official position on the house, which still stands as a chapel. The chapel has been visited by several Popes.

# Miracles and Martyrs

Faith makes miracles happen. Miracles do not make faith happen. Let me explain: think of all the miracles Jesus performed while with us. Remember his first miracle, changing the water into wine at Cana. When Mary noticed that the wine was low, she wanted to help and prevent an embarrassment to the wedding party. She asked Jesus to intervene. Jesus told her, "Woman, my time has not yet come. Mary then says to the servants, "Do whatever He says."

Jesus turns the six jars of water into wine. Many people saw the powers of Jesus at the wedding. The important point at Cana was that Jesus fulfilled his mother's wishes. Even though he was not ready to begin his ministry, he honored his mother's request. Remember Cana when you think about the Blessed Mother's intercessory powers. Mary was and is the closest human being to Jesus Christ. She can intercede and amplify every request we make to the Lord. Cana proves it!

A reading of the New Testament captures many of Jesus's miracles, but not all of them. Many people were cured of their afflictions. The crippled walked, the blind were given their sight, the deaf were given their hearing, demons were driven out of people, and the dead were raised. Despite all these visible miracles, many still did not believe that Jesus was the Son of God. They saw, but did not comprehend or believe. They heard the words, but did not understand the meaning of the words that Jesus was trying to convey.

The early Christians were persecuted by the Romans, as were the Jews. Many people went to their death defending their faith. Dying for your faith is called martyrdom in the Catholic Church. All but one of Jesus's twelve apostles were martyred. Only the Apostle John died a natural death.

When Dana, Kerrie, and I visited Rome in 2003, we went to the Colosseum. The remains of this structure are still very much intact. You can view the area where the gladiators fought and the mock battles took place. The emperor, to keep peace in the empire, provided entertainment to the people by "blood sport." Watching people die was entertainment in Rome. The movie *Gladiator* accurately depicts the violence.

As I looked down from the remnants of the stadium seats to the arena floor, I was overcome with compassion. In my imagination, I saw entire families screaming for mercy. Wild beasts tore apart Christian family members in that arena. I cannot even comprehend the fear and pain these early Christians experienced.

But maybe the Lord gave each one of them unfathomable courage at their moment of death. Maybe he put them in a state where others heard their screams, but internally they were all at peace and not suffering. Maybe in their last moments on this earth, they saw the Kingdom of God and our Blessed Mother welcoming all of them home.

The sacrifices made by early Christians should never be forgotten by any of us. It strengthens our faith and attests to the power of the early church. The human side of our Lord suffered great fear and trepidation in the Garden of

Gethsemane the night before He was crucified. He was so afraid of His crucifixion and the pain He would have to endure, He sweat blood all night. He was all alone. The other apostles fell asleep and did not pray with Him as He had requested. Yes, He was Divine, but God wanted the human side of our Lord to pay the ultimate price so that our sins could be forgiven. Jesus was the essence of love, purity, and human perfection. His death was the perfect and final sacrifice to give each of us a pathway to Heaven.

To be a martyr, one must endure their own Gethsemane. In the defining moments of their lives, martyrs do not deny God and endure unfathomable suffering. They each must overcome human fear with a faith that very few of us on Earth will ever possess. That is why they are saints. The rest of us need to look to their example and never forget the power of our own faith.

Faith gives us great strength at the moment of death. Saint Peter denied the Lord three times on Good Friday, as Jesus predicted. He later went on to be the first Pope and lead the church until he, too, was crucified. Think about that. He is filled with fear and says he does not know the Lord three times. Then a few decades later, he goes to his death willingly for the faith. He asks his captors to turn his cross upside down. He does not want his death compared to our Lord's crucifixion. A reading of church history will provide details of the horrific suffering and deaths of eleven of the twelve apostles. Each one died defending our Lord and the Catholic faith.

Saint Peter's courage attests to the power of Christianity. I believe the last martyrs have not been born yet. Many more Christians will have to defend their faith in the years to come. Our Christian faith is under attack now and will be in the foreseeable future. Remember, bars stayed open, and churches had to close during the COVID lockdown. Prophetic!

Queen of the Most Holy Rosary

Queen of the Saints

Queen of Peace

Mother of Our Savior

Mother of the Church

Mother Most Pure

Lady of Sorrows

# The Rosary

*Realize the power in your hand with the Rosary, for in your hands you hold the power of God. If you do not recognize the Rosary, can you expect to be recognized by My Son? How much can you expect? Why do you hide my Rosary? It was with a Mother's loving heart that I chose to give you these pearls of Heaven that you reject.*

*Woe to all dedicated who seek to remove these from the little ones' hands, for their punishment will be metered in accordance to it!*

*Why has sophisticated man cast aside these tokens of my love? Those who remain true to my Rosary will not be touched by the fires. Gather these treasures, my children, for the time will come that you will not find them on the counters of your stores.*

—Our Lady of the Roses, October 6 1970

For Catholics, saying the Rosary is a powerful weapon to combat the Devil. The only more powerful weapon is receiving Holy Communion at Mass.

The Rosary's origin was the result of a Marian apparition to Saint Dominic. In the year 1214, Saint Dominic was suffering from depression because he was failing to convert a group of heretics (nonbelievers who desecrated Church teachings) to Christianity. He went alone into the forest and prayed continuously for three days. He fasted this entire time and finally fell into a coma.

Dominic experienced an apparition of the Blessed Mother while in his coma. The Immaculate Mary, with three angels, appeared and asked St. Dominic, "Dear Dominic, do you know which weapon the Blessed Trinity (God the Father, God the Son (Jesus) and God the Holy Spirit) wants to use to reform the world?" Dominic did not know and asked the Blessed Mother for her guidance.

Mary responded, "I want you to know that, in this kind of warfare, the battering ram has always been the Angelic Psalter, which is the foundation stone of the New Testament. Therefore, if you want to reach these hardened souls and win them over to God, preach my Psalter." A Psalter refers to the Book of Psalms. There is a relationship between King David's Psalms in the Old Testament and the mysteries of the Rosary.

Shortly after this apparition, Dominic started preaching the Holy Rosary to the heretics. He identified fifteen mysteries from the New Testament and grouped them into three sets of five decades each. Each decade consisted of the Our Father prayer, the Glory Be prayer, and the Hail Mary prayer.

The mysteries, or Bible stories, were the way Saint Dominic educated the heretics on Jesus's teachings in the New Testament. Saint Dominic preached the Rosary for the rest of his life. He preached it by his example, as well as by his sermons to Catholics and heretics alike.

The Old Testament records the relationship between God and the Jewish people, also known as the Chosen People. The Old Testament's bible stories are not mentioned in the

Rosary. Why? Moses received the Ten Commandments from God. God established a covenant with his Chosen People. Prophets in the Old Testament prophesized the forthcoming of a Messiah. The Messiah was to be the promised deliverer (Savior) of the Jewish nation prophesied in the Hebrew Bible.

The New Testament is the fulfillment of God's promises contained in the Old Testament. Jesus is the Messiah promised by God, and the New Testament records the life and words of Jesus Christ. Simple enough, right? Not so fast. The Jewish people accept Jesus as a prophet, but not his Divinity. They do not believe him to be the promised Messiah. Muslims believe the same; that Jesus was a prophet, but not God. Interestingly enough, Muslims hold our Blessed Mother in very high regard.

To the Muslims, the Blessed Mother is the true *sayyida*, or lady. The only serious rivals to Mary in Islam are Mohammed's daughter, Fatima, and his wife. Mary is viewed by Muslims as one of the four greatest women in Islamic history. Fatima, Portugal is the site of our Blessed Mother's appearance in 1917. The town was named when the Moor (Muslim) lords invaded and ruled Portugal in the twelfth century.

The groupings of the Rosary were designated as Joyous Mysteries, Sorrowful Mysteries, and Glorious Mysteries. Five more mysteries were added by Saint Pope John Paul II in 2002. We call these the Luminous Mysteries. In appendix B I have listed all the mysteries, along with the Bible passage which refers to each mystery.

All the Rosary mysteries were attended by our Blessed Mother except the Agony of the Garden, The Proclamation of the Kingdom, and the Transfiguration of our Lord.

Sister Lùcia, one of three children to see our Lady at Fatima, Portugal in 1917, became a nun and devoted her life to the Lord. She died at the age of ninety-seven. While she was alive, many religious leaders interviewed her and asked for clarification of the Fatima secrets revealed to her by our Blessed Mother. In an interview in 1957, Sister Lùcia said this about the power of the Rosary:

*. . . The decadence which exists in the world is without any doubt the consequence of the lack of the spirit of prayer. Foreseeing this disorientation, the Blessed Virgin recommended recitation of the Rosary with such insistence. And since the Rosary is, after the holy Eucharistic liturgy, the prayer most apt for preserving faith in souls, the Devil has unchained his struggles against it. Unfortunately, we see the disasters he has caused.*

*. . . We must defend souls against the errors which can make them stray from the good road. We cannot and we must not stop ourselves, nor allow, as Our Lord says, the children of Darkness to be wiser than the children of Light . . . The Rosary is the most powerful weapon for defending ourselves on the field of battle.*

# Mary at the Crossroads of History

A few years back, Father Francis (Rocky) Hoffman wrote a book about the impact our Blessed Mother has had on the history of the world. Father Hoffman is a gifted writer. He explains concepts and facts so that even the younger kids can understand key points. In the case of explaining faith to others, simple is good. When we try to complicate our faith and intellectualize it, some of us can get lost.

Father Rocky talks about inflection points in our Christian history—moments in time that change the direction of civilizations and cultures. He cites several events in our history where our Blessed Mother's intervention dramatically altered the outcome of world history.

Here is one example he uses: Spain was once ruled by the Muslim Caliphate in the seventh century. In fact, the Muslims ruled Spain until the fourteen hundreds, for over seven hundred years. The Muslim Empire stretched from modern day Syria and Turkey and included most of the old Roman Empire surrounding the Mediterranean Sea.

In 722, Spain was completely overrun by the Muslims. Many Christians were horribly slaughtered, and the last remaining fighting forces retreated into the mountains of Northern Spain. It was a desperate situation for the Christians. As we would say in the Marine Corps, they were outnumbered and outgunned. The Muslims had the newest weapons and tactics; the Christians had rocks and logs. It was a horrible mismatch.

The leader of the Christians was a man named Pelagius. You might say that he and his forces did not have a prayer. The stakes were high. If the Muslim forces defeated his small mountain militia forces, there was nothing stopping them from overrunning southern France and all of Europe. As the situation grew more desperate, Pelagius went to pray in the Holy Cave of Covadonga, where there was an image of the Blessed Mother.

The Muslim forces closed in on the Christians. The Muslim archers began firing their arrows, but something strange happened. The arrows ricocheted off the mountain rocks, striking the Muslim soldiers.

Encouraged by what had to be a miracle, Pelagius and his men let their rocks and logs roll down the mountainside, crushing the Muslims. Then God showed up!

A violent rainstorm caused intense flooding, and a landslide crushed many more Muslim soldiers. Unbelievable? No, it was the intervention of our Blessed Mother and her Son in a time of crisis. The Muslim force retreated. The Reconquista, or Reconquering, of Spain had begun. It would take seven hundred and eighty-one years to get the job done, but Christianity was saved and now had a chance to flourish in Europe.

Another inflection point in history Father Rocky uses involves our Blessed Mother and the voyages of Christopher

Columbus. We all learned in school, at least we should have learned, that Columbus was trying to discover a new route to the Far East, when his forces landed on modern day Haiti. He was funded by King Ferdinand and Queen Isabella of Spain.

Columbus had studied the journals of Marco Polo who, two hundred years earlier, had discovered an overland route to the Indies (modern day India and China). Marco went east from Italy and traveled overland across Asia to reach the western edge of present-day China. In his journals, he mentioned that the Great Khan (King of China) had requested that Marco bring more men of the faith to teach him more about Christianity. Marco said in his journal that he did ask the Pope to fulfill Khan's request, but the Pope did not act on it.

When Columbus got his audience with the king and queen, he told them about the Great Khan's request to learn more about the faith. Ferdinand and Isabella funded the voyage in part because they wanted to bring Christianity to the people of the Indies. Of course, there were financial gains to be had. But the king and queen were both driven by their devotion to the Blessed Mother and the spreading of the Catholic faith. Remember it is 1492, before Protestantism came about through the efforts of Father Martin Luther, a Catholic priest. Christianity was the Catholic faith; no other Christian sects existed at the time of Columbus's voyages.

When he finally did sail with his three ships, one named the Santa Maria (Saint Mary), he encountered many challenges. He got stuck in the doldrums halfway across the Atlantic. The doldrums are a scientific phenomenon in the Atlantic

Ocean where there is intense heat and no wind. Many ships were lost at sea in the doldrums. Columbus's ships all stopped dead in the sea. The crew was running out of water. Finally, after praying to the Blessed Mother, the wind came up and the ships began moving.

On October 12th Columbus landed on the island of Hispaniola, modern-day Dominican Republic and Haiti. October 12th was celebrated here in the USA for many years, until Columbus became cancelled. We now call Columbus Day Indigenous Peoples' Day. There is a whole background story to this change, but we should never forget the courage it took to command three ships across an ocean that no one had dared to travel. We should remember that it was this first voyage that initially planted the seeds of Christianity in the New World.

Another interesting fact is that October 12th is also celebrated in Spain, in memory of Our Lady of Pillar. Here is the story: When Saint James the apostle was in Spain trying to convert the Spaniards to Christianity in the first century, he was almost ready to quit when Our Blessed Mother appeared to him. She was still alive and lived in Ephesus at the time with Saint John. She convinced him, through an apparition, to stay the course and to remember that if he converted the Spaniards to the faith, they would take it all around the world. Spain did so through the voyages of Columbus, Magellan, and others. Coincidence? I do not think so—the Blessed Mother at work for sure.

On the way back from his first voyage, Columbus encountered a tremendous storm. Many men panicked and thought they would all be lost at sea. The storm lasted for several days. Columbus ordered his men to pray to the Blessed Mother, which they did. Columbus also promised that if they survived the storm, one of the crew would make a special visit to Our Lady of Guadalupe, a holy site in Spain.

A lottery was conducted to determine who would make the pilgrimage. Columbus drew the winning chickpea. He did visit the site and thanked the Blessed Mother. This was his second visit to the shrine of Our Lady of Guadalupe. On the first visit two years earlier, he met representatives of King Ferdinand and Queen Isabella, who arranged a meeting between Columbus and the royal couple. This meeting resulted in the funding for Columbus's voyages. Coincidence? I think not. Once again, our Blessed Mother has and will have a profound impact on human history.

Father Rocky's book has many other examples of our Blessed Mother's influence on human events. Perhaps her greatest impacts on our world were her apparitions, especially those in Fatima, Portugal in 1917. I will talk about what happened at Fatima later.

# Consolations

Let me turn now to the ways Jesus and Mary reveal themselves in our lives and console us here on Earth.

We all have ups and downs in life. It is seldom a smooth ride, and we hit lots of potholes and ruts. If we become increasingly gloomy and self-obsessed, we are being actively attacked by the "Evil One." We call this desolation, a term first used by Saint Ignatius of Loyola. Desolation drains our energy, causes us to think only about ourselves, causes anxiety, and can lead to depression.

In contrast to desolation, a consolation is feeling the presence of the Lord in a positive way. A consolation can come in the form of a feeling or an event. The Holy Spirit often uses our Blessed Mother to deliver a consolation to us.

My most recent consolation experience came to me when I visited a dying friend. We had known each other for several years and attended the same mass on many occasions. Pat lost her husband of forty-five years, Joe, about the same time we lost our son, John, in 2017.

On her death bed, we had a chance to talk. She was at peace. I asked her to remember my son when she arrived in Heaven. My remarks and feelings seemed almost childlike to me. Pat completely understood my feelings, and said she would see Joe and John in Heaven. There was such a feeling of peace I experienced at that moment. It was a consolation from our

Lord. A consolation is a way our Lord and his mother remind us that they are "on the job," watching out for us and listening to our prayers. Consolations remind all of us that there is something bigger than this life waiting for us. Consolations bring us hope.

About a week after Pat's death her daughter, Patty, came to my house to talk about her mom's last moments on Earth. I had previously given Patty a Divine Mercy card and asked her to place it on the pillow near her mom's head. She told me she did so and, in addition, she had prayed the Divine Mercy Chaplet with her mom moments before her death. She told me her mother was at peace in her last moments. Jesus promised to Saint Faustina that all those who prayed the Divine Mercy Chaplet would not experience terror in the last moments of life. Jesus's promise was certainly true in Pat's case.

Another recent consolation I received was at my grandson's First Holy Communion. The entire family was in the church as Michael and the other children walked down the aisle with reverently folded hands. As I looked on, I remembered my son John's First Holy Communion in 1983. I have a picture of John holding his Rosary and prayer book. I look at this picture a lot. It reminds me that John was loaned to me by God. All children are loaned to their parents. They all belong to God. John and Michael both belong to God.

As I looked at the faces of all the young children coming down the aisle, I could not help but feel gratitude for the life God has given me. I have been blessed with many gifts. The sweet and innocent faces of Michael's classmates reinforced to me the power of love. The beaming faces of all the parents and grandparents in the church amplified this love.

Love is the greatest gift God gives us. Love and hope can conquer any challenge in our lives. I was consoled in that church, and I know others felt the same sense of faith that I did. Too bad we cannot all stay children, where trust is an everyday occurrence.

We trust our parents and teachers. As we grow older, we sometimes grow more cynical. It is harder to just accept the simple gifts of life. We tend to complicate our lives with clutter. Children keep things simple, like trusting that the Holy Eucharist is the body and blood of our Lord.

Saying the Rosary is a powerful way to keep the Devil at bay and remain close to Christ. The Rosary is a way to reflect on your blessings and ask the Lord for your special intentions. As you say the Hail Mary, Our Father, Glory Be, or Apostles Creed, you reaffirm and strengthen your faith.

Prayer can positively influence every aspect of your life. Many saints have dedicated their entire lives to praying to our Blessed Mother and doing good works in her honor. Saint Louis de Montfort was one of them.

# Total Consecration to Mary

Saint Louis de Montfort was an eighteenth-century Catholic missionary. He wrote a book on the Blessed Virgin, titled *True Devotion to the Blessed Virgin*, in 1712. His devotion to our Blessed Mary is something referred to as "Marian" devotion.

Father Montfort's approach to Marian devotion was simple; Jesus and Mary are inseparable. He views devotion to Mary as a special path to being united to Christ, given that:

*. . . of all creatures the one most conformed to Jesus Christ, it follows that among all devotions that which most consecrates and conforms a soul to our Lord is devotion to Mary, his Holy Mother, and that the more a soul is consecrated to her the more will it be consecrated to Jesus Christ.*

*God the Father made an assemblage of all the waters, and He named it the sea (mare). He has made an assemblage of all His graces, and He has called it Mary (Maria).*

In Saint Louis de Montfort's view, we all need to surrender ourselves to Jesus through Mary and perform all actions "with Mary, in Mary, through Mary, and for Mary." He, too, believed the Rosary was a powerful means to stay in touch with our Blessed Mother, thereby becoming closer to her son.

Saint John Vianney was another saint I have come to know since John died in 2017. Saint John grew up around the time of the French Revolution and the reign of Napoleon Bonaparte.

He escaped being drafted in the French Army and found his great calling to the priesthood in the mountains.

He was not the brightest academic, but he persevered and finally became a parish priest in 1818. He was very strict in his application of the Catholic faith. Many Catholics were not practicing their faith in the town of Ars, where Saint John lived. Many had completely forgotten the basics of their faith, since the practice of Catholicism was outlawed during and after the French Revolution. Saint John had a terrific challenge and, through his dogged determination, brought his Ars parishioners back to their faith.

He spent at least twelve hours a day in the confessional during winter, and up to sixteen in the summer. The following story exemplifies the great faith and spiritual insights of this simple parish priest:

*. . . a woman . . . told . . . Vianney that she was devastated because her husband had committed suicide. She wanted to approach the great priest, but his confessional line often lasted for hours and she could not reach him. She was ready to give up and in a moment of mystical insight that only a great saint can receive . . . Vianney exclaimed through the crowd, He is saved! The woman was incredulous, so the saint repeated, stressing each word, I tell you he is saved. He is in purgatory, and you must pray for him. Between the parapet of the bridge and the water, he had time to make an act of contrition.*

This story is very consoling to me, as the father of a son who took his life. John is with me every moment of every day. He needs my prayers. For whatever reason, John took his life on the 10th of January, 2017. I pray for his soul every day. I have faith that Saint John Vianney and all the saints are also praying for him.

It is prayer that sustains me. I have nothing in my life that is more important than praying to the Lord and His Blessed Mother for the repose of my son and all those who have passed on from this life to the next. I try to view my faith through the eyes of a child. I trust in the teachings of my church. God never leaves us, even in the closing moments of our earthly life. If you believe in a merciful Jesus, and I do, it makes perfect sense that He will open the gates of his mercy if we are repentant. I believe my son had time in the last milliseconds of his life to love the Lord as he had as a child. I believe John is on his way to Heaven.

Jesus and His mother offer each of us mercy and forgiveness in the darkest moments of our lives. When everything around us is shattered and broken, the light of our Lord and the prayers of his Blessed Mother defeat the "Evil One" and give us all hope.

Saint John Vianney also had a great devotion to our Blessed Mother. His prayer to Mary includes the following verses:

*. . . Help me especially in my last hours. Help me overcome the evil spirits. Stay with me when I stand in judgment before your Son. If I have to do penance for my sins in purgatory, pray for me after my death. Inspire my friends to pray for me. Lead my soul to Heaven where, united with the elect, I may bless and praise God and yourself for all eternity. Amen.*

Both the saints I have discussed, Fathers Louis de Montfort and John Vianney, had a special devotion to the "Immaculate Heart of Mary." The Immaculate Heart of Mary symbolizes the purity of Mary and her complete fidelity to God. As the vessel for our Lord, Mary's heart had to reflect all the goodness of our world. Her Immaculate Heart is also a heart pierced with sorrow. Mary's Immaculate Heart reflects selflessness, sacrifice, love, and loyalty. It is untainted by any worldly defect. It is sinless and pure and is the most pleasing heart to our Lord in all of humanity.

As I have said earlier, Mary is a powerful intercessor. She can magnify our prayers, especially for our deceased loved ones. I know that some reading this book do not believe in the concept of Purgatory or praying for the dead, but let me just make a couple of points here.

First, Catholics believe that Purgatory is a gift. It is a place of suffering, where all of one's imperfections are burned away to allow each of us to be perfected. Nothing imperfect goes through Heaven's gate. To look upon the Beatific Vision of the Lord one must be perfected, thus Purgatory gives us a gateway to Heaven. Without Purgatory, Hell would be the only option for those of us who failed to reach perfection here on Earth. Thank God for Purgatory!

Our prayers to the Blessed Mother, especially the Rosary, are the surest way to help release the souls in Purgatory. If you are in Purgatory, you are going to Heaven. I can't answer any of the big questions, like how much time one spends in Purgatory, but I do know that God is outside of time. A lifetime here on Earth could be but a mere second in God's time. It is a mystery. God's plan will be revealed to us when He decides to do so. So, I pray every day for the dead, especially for family members and friends.

Can Mary really appear to people here on Earth? Are Marian apparitions a reality, or just the made-up visions of people who want attention? Can the spiritual world really come to Earth? The short answer to all these questions is YES!

# Marian Apparitions

An apparition is the appearance of a "being," normally invisible to human sight. As mortals, we cannot see Mary's "glorified body" in her Assumption. Through God's power a representation of Mary can appear, which is visible to the eyes of one or more people.

Even in our day, there are many reports of apparitions of Mary throughout the world. The Catholic Church admits there can be apparitions, but a process of discernment is necessary to make an appearance of our Blessed Mother "worthy of belief." Even when the Church gives its approval of an apparition, the Church does not require that we believe them. The Church believes, however, that if Mary appears at a particular time and place, it is because she wants us to listen more attentively to what her Son has said or done for our salvation.

The spiritual benefits from an apparition of Mary have been powerful. Entire nations have converted to Christianity and become closer to Jesus, as in the case of our Lady of Guadalupe in Mexico. After her appearance millions of people converted to Christianity. Millions of people today wear the Miraculous Medal because of Mary's appearance to Saint Catherine Labourè. The Berlin Wall came down, and communism collapsed because of our Lady of Fatima's appearance in 1917, and the subsequent consecration of Russia to her Sacred Heart by Saint John Paul II.

I will not cover all the Marian apparitions in this writing. Volumes have been written on the subject, but I would like to comment on four apparitions. Before I do, let me tell you about my "near apparition."

It was during my first trip to Ireland. I can still see all the shades of green in the country of my family's origin. We were near County Cork. I got up early for one of my usual runs. I was in the Marine Corps at the time, and I ran almost every day.

It was quite foggy that morning in early June 2000. I started running down an old country road. I went for about two miles and then turned around. It was cool and crisp, but the fog kept me from seeing anything more than a hundred feet away. It was a soupy type of fog—thick and dense.

As I rounded a corner, I saw in the distance who I believed to be the Virgin Mary. She had a white gown on and a veil that went down below her shoulders. Her dress was long and her hands were outstretched. I kept saying to myself, "this cannot be real. It must be an apparition."

I slowed down to try to figure out what I was seeing. I was confused. As I got closer, Mary got bigger. She was off the road a little, along what I believed to be a hillside. I started to tear-up. The apparition seemed so real to me. I felt a spirit I cannot describe. I convinced myself, as I got closer to the apparition, I was having an out-of-body experience.

About twenty feet away, I stopped and starting walking toward the Blessed Mother. She seemed to be inside of a structure. There were flowers strewn along her feet. Finally, when I got about ten feet away, I realized this was not a dream, not an apparition, but rather a statue of Mary located inside a small cave. I was relieved that I was not just seeing things. The statue was real.

The Irish are known for a fervent devotion to Mary and there are many statues of her throughout Ireland, in churches and in various hidden places as well. So that is my Virgin Mary story. Let us keep talking about Ireland. The first apparition I would like to talk about is Our Lady of Knock.

# Our Lady of Knock

Saint Patrick is the patron saint of Ireland and is responsible for helping convert the early Irish nonbelievers to Catholicism. In the fourth century, he used the shamrock to explain the Trinity to the Druids in Ireland. The shamrock is a three-leaf plant. Saint Patrick pointed to the shamrock leaf and said, "One God in three divine persons—Father, Son, and Holy Spirit."

The Catholic tradition in Ireland remains strong. However, the internal strife between Protestants and Catholics on the "Emerald Island" has been fierce over the centuries. The English occupied the island for many decades.

During the 1840s the Great Potato Famine occurred. Over two million Irish men, women, and children starved to death. Their English overlords did not send in food supplies to alleviate the suffering. Hatred developed. One thing that did grow among the Irish people was their faith. Irish Catholics prayed to Mary throughout the famine, with a profound devotion to her and her intercessory powers.

On the evening of August 21, 1879 Mary McLoughlin, the housekeeper to the parish priest of Knock, was astonished to see the outside south wall of the church glowing in a mysterious light. There were three figures standing in front of the wall. Mary initially thought these figures were the replacements for the stone figures destroyed by a recent storm. But she needed to have her visions validated by someone else. She rushed through the rain to the house of her friend, Margaret Byrne.

After a half hour, Mary decided to leave, and Margaret's sister Mary agreed to walk Margaret home. As they passed the church, they saw an amazing vision. Standing out to the west of the church near the wall appeared the Blessed Virgin, St. Joseph, and St. John. The figure of the Blessed Virgin was life-size, while the others seemed a bit smaller. These figures stood a little away from the wall and about two feet off the ground. The Virgin was erect, with her eyes set toward Heaven. She was wearing a large white cloak hanging in full folds, and on her head was a large crown.

Mary Byrne ran to tell her family. Mary McLoughlin continued to gaze at the apparition. Soon a crowd gathered and everyone saw the apparition. Among the witnesses were Patrick Hill and John Curry. Patrick later described the scene: "The figures were fully rounded, as if they had a body and life. They did not speak and as we drew near, they retreated a little toward the wall." Patrick reported that he got close enough to make out the words in the book held by the figure of St. John.

The next day a group of villagers went to see the parish priest. He believed their report and wrote to the Bishop of Tuam. The church set up a commission to interview several people who claimed to have witnessed the apparition. The church hierarchy was not convinced, and some members of the commission ridiculed the visionaries, saying they were victims of a hoax made by local Protestants. But the ordinary

Irish people believed the apparition and pilgrimages to Knock began in 1880. In 1882, Archbishop John Joseph Lynch of Toronto made a visit to the parish and claimed he had been healed by the Virgin of Knock.

Over the years, many of the witnesses died. Mary Byrne married, raised six children, and lived her entire life in Knock. When interviewed in 1936 at the age of eighty-six, her account did not vary from the first report she gave in 1879.

The village of Knock was transformed. Thousands came to commemorate the vision and to ask for healing for others and themselves. The local church was too small to accommodate the crowds. In 1976 a new church, Our Lady Queen of Ireland, was erected. It holds more than two thousand people. Each year Knock receives more than half a million visitors who come to pay their respects to the Blessed Virgin.

The Catholic Church approved the apparition at Knock in 1971 as being "quite probable." The shrine at Knock is open year-round. In 1994, three life-sized statues were erected of Our Lady, Saint Joseph, and Saint John.

I believe there is great significance to both Saint John and Saint Joseph appearing with our Blessed Mother in the apparition. Both of these earthly men took care of our Blessed Mother. Don't forget that Saint John was the only apostle at the foot of the Cross. It was John who took care of our Blessed Mother after the Resurrection of our Lord. It was Saint John who wrote the Book of Revelation in the New Testament, where he sees the Virgin as "Queen of Heaven and Earth."

## The Miraculous Medal

I have worn the Miraculous Medal for many years. Let me tell you the story behind the medal. Before I do, please keep in mind that Catholic medals are sacramentals. Statues, medals, and paintings are all forms of sacramentals. We do not pray to the sacramentals; we pray to whom and what they represent. My Miraculous Medal has the figure of Mary engraved on it. This medal reminds me of the special intercessory powers of our Blessed Mother.

Catherine Labouré was born on May 2, 1806 in the Burgundy region of France. Her parents owned a small farm. She was the ninth of eleven children. Labouré's mother died on October 9, 1815 when Catherine was just nine years old. It is said that after her mother's funeral, Catherine picked up a statue of the Blessed Virgin Mary and kissed it, saying, "Now you will be my mother."

Her father's sister offered to care for Catherine and her sisters and they moved to Saint-Rémy. It is there that Catherine had a dream of a priest who said to her: "My daughter, it is good to care for the sick. For now, you flee from me, but one day you will be glad to approach me. God has plans for you. Don't forget it!" Later in life, Catherine recognized the priest as Saint Vincent de Paul.

At the age of twelve, Catherine returned to her father's farm to help care for her family. Her father did not want her to pursue a religious life and sent her to Paris to work in his brothers' eating establishment for poor workers. While working in this shelter, she was greatly affected by the suffering of the poor. She made her decision to enter the nursing order of Saint Vincent de Paul, the Daughters of Charity.

She studied to be a nun at a convent in Paris and she took her vows in 1831. Catherine stated that on July 19, 1830, on the eve of the feast of St. Vincent de Paul, she awoke hearing the voice of a child calling out to her in the chapel. While in the chapel, she heard the Virgin Mary say to her, "God wishes to charge you with a mission. You will be contradicted, but do not fear; you will have the grace to do what is necessary. Tell your spiritual director all that passes within you. Times are evil in France and in the world."

On November 27, 1830, Catherine reported that Mary appeared to her during her evening meditations. She displayed herself inside an oval frame, standing upon a globe. Rays of light came out of her hands in the direction of the globe. Around the margin of the frame appeared the words "O Mary, conceived without sin, pray for us who have recourse to thee."

Catherine watched as the frame seemed to rotate, showing a circle of twelve stars, a large letter *M* surmounted by a cross, and the stylized Sacred Heart of Jesus and Immaculate Heart of Mary underneath. Asked why some of the rays of light did not reach the earth, Mary reportedly replied, "Those are the graces for which people forget to ask." Mary then asked her to take these images to her priest, telling him that they should be put on medallions. Mary told her, "All who wear them will receive great graces."

Catherine told her priest about her vision and the Blessed Mother's instructions. After two years of investigation and observation of her daily behavior, the priest took the information to his archbishop. He did not reveal Catherine's identity.

The request was approved and the design of the medallion was commissioned. The medals proved to be extremely popular with Catholics and were quickly adopted by millions. The Medal also played an important role in the announcement by Pope Pius IX that the first feast day of the "Immaculate Conception" would be celebrated on December 8, 1854. Catholics have celebrated this feast day ever since.

During combat operations in the Marine Corps, I wore my Miraculous Medal. I always felt the Blessed Mother was looking out for me. I prayed the Hail Mary many times during my deployments. My dad also wore his Miraculous Medal in air combat operations during World War II and the Korean War. Both Dad and I believed that the Blessed Virgin was always there to help protect us.

# Saint Faustina's Visions of Mary

Saint Faustina was a Polish nun who was visited by Jesus in the 1930s. Really? Yes, and the Catholic Church made her a saint and her diary is now considered divinely inspired by the church. In this diary, Sister Faustina wrote down all the things Jesus said to her.

Jesus gave Saint Faustina two tasks: one, to paint a picture of him as he appeared to her. There is now such a portrait in most Catholic churches. The second task Jesus gave to Saint Faustina was to write a prayer, which would remind the world of his "unfathomable mercy." Look up the Chaplet of Divine Mercy on the internet. It is usually prayed at three in the afternoon, which is believed to be the hour Christ died on his cross. Jesus also directed Saint Faustina to write the following words at the bottom of his portrait, "Jesus, I trust in you." The chaplet prayer includes the words, "For the sake of his sorrowful passion, have mercy on us and the whole world." The Chaplet, said in combination with the Rosary, are the most powerful prayers in my opinion. We are calling on Jesus and His mother to heal our troubled souls and bring us grace to persevere in this life.

Saint Faustina is most often associated with her revelations of the merciful Jesus, not so much with the ones she experienced with the Blessed Mother. However, she experienced many revelations by our Blessed Mother. While Mother Mary talked with Sister Faustina, Mary revealed to her the mystery of Divine Mercy in her own life. She said to Faustina, "Out of the depths of God's Mercy, I am your mother and I am not only the Queen of Heaven, but also the mother of mercy and your mother."

No human being has ever received the daily attention from the Blessed Mother as Saint Faustina experienced. It was Our Lady who told Saint Faustina that her divine mercy mission would be to prepare the world for Christ's final coming. On the first of May 1933, the day of her perpetual vows, Saint Faustina addressed Mary and prayed, "*Mother of God, most holy Mary, my mother, you are my mother in a special way because your beloved son is now my bridegroom, and thus we are both your children. For your son's sake, you have to love me. O Mary, my dearest mother, guide my whole life in such a way that it will always please your son, Jesus.*"

Saint Faustina's prayer was answered. Mary appeared to her and said: "My daughter, at God's command I will be with you in a special and exclusive way, and you will be my special daughter, but I desire that you, too, be my child in a special way."

Perhaps the most powerful entry in Saint Faustina's diary was the following:

*I saw the Mother of God who said to me, "Oh, how pleasing to God is the soul that follows faithfully the inspirations of His grace! I gave the Savior to the world; as for you, you have to speak to the world about his great mercy and prepare the world for the second coming of him who will come, not as a merciful Savior, but as a just judge. Oh, how terrible is that day! Determined is the day of justice, the day of Divine wrath. The angels tremble before it. Speak to souls about this great mercy while it is still the time for mercy. If you keep silent now, you will be answering for a great number of souls on that terrible day. Fear nothing. Be faithful to the end. I sympathize with you."*

After John died in 2017, I was introduced to the concept of Divine Mercy. I really embraced the words, "before I come as a just judge, I come as a merciful judge." According to Saint Faustina's revelations, when our soul passes from this life, Jesus comes to it and asks the soul to accept him and his mercy. He comes three times to our souls. If, on his third attempt, our soul refuses to accept him, it cannot be saved. Jesus also mentions to Saint Faustina that prayers are timeless. Jesus is outside of time. Our prayers can go back in time and help our loved one accept the Lord. This is a very comforting revelation to me. I pray a lot for my loved ones, especially for our John.

I read all six-hundred pages of Saint Faustina's diary a few years back. I still read parts of it today. I concentrated on the words Jesus spoke to her. I never took into account all the times our Blessed Mother spoke to Saint Faustina. I now have a greater appreciation for the words our Mother spoke to Faustina. She interceded for her Son and emphasized the second coming of our Lord. She declared herself to be the Mother of Mercy, and she warns the world that we should all accept our merciful Savior before He comes as a just judge. To a Christian, this should be an attention gainer for sure.

# Our Lady of Fatima, 1917

***O my Jesus take away our sins, save us from the fires of Hell, bring all souls to Heaven, especially those in most need of your mercy.***

The above prayer is one of the prayers we say during the Rosary. It was given to the world by our Blessed Mother at Fatima, Portugal. Our Lady appeared six times to three children in Fatima in 1917. Lùcia dos Santos and her two cousins, Francisco and Jacinta, were tending sheep in a village outside the village of Fatima. A flash of lightning drew their attention to a tree. Above the tree, they saw a lady dressed in white standing on a cloud.

Our Lady of Fatima warned the children that God would further punish the world for its disobedience to His will by war, hunger, and the persecution of the Church. The Blessed Virgin prophesied that Russia would be God's chosen "instrument of chastisement, spreading the errors of atheism and materialism across the earth, fomenting wars, annihilating nations, and persecuting the faithful everywhere." That is exactly what happened with the rise of communism and the Cold War in the twentieth century.

In all her appearances at Fatima, the Blessed Mother repeatedly emphasized the necessity of praying the Rosary daily, wearing the Brown Scapular of Mount Carmel, and for all of us to perform acts of "reparation and sacrifice." Our Lady requested a solemn and public "consecration of Russia to her Immaculate Heart" by the Pope and all the Catholic bishops of the world. She also asked that the "faithful" practice a new devotion of reparation(penance) and to attend Mass on the first Saturday of five consecutive months. We call these "the Five First Saturdays."

The central theme of Our Lady's message to the world is contained in what has been called the "secret," which Mary confided to the three children. The secret consists of three parts, which have all been publicly revealed.

The first part of the secret was a horrifying vision of Hell, "where the souls of poor sinners go." Mary told the children that acts of prayer and sacrifice were necessary to save souls. "You have seen Hell, where the souls of poor sinners go. It is to save them that God wants to establish devotion in the world to my Immaculate Heart. If you do what I tell you, many souls will be saved, and there will be peace."

It is good to reflect on Hell. Why? You could be heading there if you do not get your life in order. What order? Simple. Start thinking about others. Start praying to the Lord for forgiveness. Accept your "broken" condition as a sinner and move in a positive direction. Get rid of your addictions, which are blocking God from entering and bringing peace to your interior self. Easy stuff, right? For some it is. For others, they would rather live a consequence-free life. Our Blessed Mother tried to warn us in 1917 that we will suffer great consequences if we turn away from her Son and her Sacred Heart.

The second part of the secret predicted the outbreak of World War II and included the request for the "consecration of Russia" as a condition for world peace. It also predicted the inevitable triumph of Mary's Immaculate Heart and the conversion of "that poor nation (Russia)" to the Faith.

Given what is going on today in Russia, some may doubt the words of the Virgin. The Soviet Union was defeated when the Berlin Wall came crashing down in 1991. But we still have a warring Russia currently destroying the country of Ukraine. Pope Francis recently re-consecrated Russia to the Sacred Heart of Mary for the second time. Earlier in 1983 Pope John Paul performed a consecration of Mary's Immaculate Heart to Russia.

We need to always remember that despite the current struggles in our world, God wins in the end and evil is defeated. Our Blessed Mother will ensure this victory by crushing the head of the serpent, Lucifer. Devotion to her Immaculate Heart and prayer are the means we have on earth to implore God for his Divine mercy and for the intercession of the Blessed Virgin to amplify our petitions.

Perhaps the most important interview concerning the Fatima secrets was with Sister Lùcia in 1957. In it, she reveals what many believe to be the most important premonition of why our world is suffering and always seems to be on the brink of disaster. Sister Lùcia spoke of the decisive battle between the Blessed Virgin and the Devil. She told a Catholic priest, Father Fuentes, the following in 1957:

*Father, the Devil is in the mood for engaging in a decisive battle against the Blessed Virgin, and the Devil knows what it is that most offends God, and which in a short space of time will gain for him the greatest number of souls. Thus, the Devil does everything to overcome souls consecrated to God, because in this way the Devil will succeed in leaving the souls of the faithful abandoned by their leaders, thereby the more easily will he seize them . . .*

*And a decisive battle is the final battle where one side will be victorious and the other side will suffer defeat. Hence from now on we must choose sides. Either we are for God or we are for the Devil; there is no other possibility. God is giving two last remedies to the world. They are the Holy Rosary and devotion to the Immaculate Heart of Mary. These are the last two remedies which signify that there will be no others.*

The third part of the secret was not publicly revealed for decades. It became the center of speculation and catastrophic predictions by many clergy, including the end of the world. On May 13, 2000, Pope John Paul II allowed the third secret to be revealed. The Vatican clergy interpreted it as follows:

*. . . The pastors of the Church will fail gravely in the duties of their office. Through their fault, consecrated souls and the faithful in great number will let themselves be seduced by pernicious errors spread everywhere. This will be the time of the decisive battle between the Blessed Virgin and the Devil. A wave of diabolical disorientation will be hurled over the world. Satan will introduce himself even to the highest summit of the Church. He will blind the minds and harden*

*the hearts of pastors. And God will deliver them to themselves as a chastisement for their refusal to obey the requests of the Immaculate Heart of Mary. This will be the great apostasy predicted for the "last times;" "the False Lamb" and "False Prophet" will betray the Church to the profit of "the Beast," according to the prophecy of the Apocalypse.*

Whoa, that got my attention! After reading the above quotes from Saint Pope John Paul II and Sister Lùcia, I am even more convinced that our Blessed Mother will always be our gateway to Jesus, and thus to Heaven. She is the key to peace in our world.

The world may have a lot of time remaining on the clock, but the "end-times" predicted in Saint John's Book of Revelation seem to be getting closer. It is the last book contained in the New Testament. For sure, our secular world is not moving toward God or in a positive direction. Guess what? It has always been infected by evil, war, famine, and human strife.

I do not make predictions. I try to live each day to the fullest. I do realize at some point everything ends, including our earthly existence and the world as we know it. Don't dwell on it, but remind yourself that nothing lasts forever, and everyone is accountable for the life God has given them.

Our souls endure throughout eternity. Eternity cannot be comprehended by most of us. We are conditioned in this life for instant gratification. We move rapidly from one task to the next. We all get caught up with our daily activities and responsibilities. That is not a bad thing. It is necessary to do what we have to do in order to support our families and make a living. But occasionally it is a good thing to reflect on the only thing that lasts forever, your soul. Souls created by God alone. Souls are accountable for all the good and bad we do on earth. It is easy to say, "there is nothing after this life." It is catastrophic for a Christian not to stay focused on the next life.

# Children of God

This phrase is thrown around a lot in churches. It is true. We all have one God and we are all His children.

Keeping things simple is a good way to lead your life. Realize your limits, and ask for help when you need it. When I was growing up there was a bestselling book called, *All I Really Need to Know I Learned in Kindergarten*. Think about it. We learn to share in kindergarten. We learn to trust our teacher and our friends in kindergarten. We hold hands when we cross the street and learn to depend on each other. There is always someone looking out and protecting us. We learn numbers and letters and all the basic building blocks to lead successful lives.

Hopefully, we emerge from our kindergarten experience with a positive attitude and respect for learning. We carry the lessons from our elementary years with us for a lifetime. Our self-image is molded in elementary school. I think about all the things I learned from Sister Mary Joseph—lessons that have stood the test of time for me. Our teachers have a tremendous impact on us.

We all grow up in a world that can be a very scary place. There is so much uncertainty and personal struggle. We suffer through tragedy, but also experience great joy in our lives. Families go through all the hard times together. Hopefully, our family values and support systems stay in place throughout our lives.

But many people and many families break apart nowadays. If we lose our family, we are left with a hole in our heart. There is a lot of loneliness in our world. We can try to fill that hole with people and other worldly distractions. But the loneliness always returns. Only God can fill this hole. This is the most important thing I have learned in this life.

We all need to grow in the application of our faith with family and friends. We need to reach out to others in their time of need. All of us need to set the example for others, through our self-determination and personal sacrifices. Each of us needs to be continually reminded that this life is just a little stop on our way to eternity. I believe if we do all these things, we will have a "safe" landing, just as Dad did during all his carrier landings.

Recently, I learned a new prayer called the Memorare. I have heard it hundreds of times on the radio station I listen to, but I never took the time to memorize it. On *Relevant Radio* they pray the Memorare to end abortion and protect human life from the moment of conception to the end of natural life. The recent overturning of *Roe v. Wade* attests to the power of this prayer to our Blessed Mother. Here are the words to the prayer:

***Remember, O most gracious Virgin Mary, that never was it known that anyone who fled to thy protection, implored thy help, or sought thine intercession was left unaided.***

***Inspired by this confidence, I fly unto thee, O Virgin of virgins, my mother; to thee do I come, before thee I stand, sinful and sorrowful. O Mother of the Word Incarnate, despise not my petitions, but in thy mercy hear and answer me.***

## Suffering

Suffering is our Lord's way of getting our attention, at least that is what a wise Irish priest told me. Pain puts things in perspective. We can all suffer emotional, physical, and mental anguish. We can all feel like no one understands our pain. "You don't understand how bad this really is." I have said these words many times, sometimes to myself and oftentimes to others. Feeling sorry for yourself is not a remedy for the pain.

When you have a toothache, you go to a dentist. If you have a meniscus tear in your knee (and I do), you go to an orthopedic doctor. It is the same with our spiritual lives. We go to Jesus and His mother when the world throws pain our way.

Pain is the great equalizer. Rich and poor, big or small, man or woman (sorry, there are only two genders, folks!), we all experience the pain that comes from living life. How we handle our pain is the real question. As you get older, the aches and pains increase. You cannot stop time or pain. Dad always said, "You deal with what's on your plate."

We all need to strive to be "quiet sufferers." Our Lord and His mother modeled quiet suffering. Both projected a calm and humble demeanor during their time with us on Earth. Both endured the pain of the crucifixion–one on the cross, the other watching her Son's slow death. Mary became our mother at the foot of the cross. Jesus redeemed all of us through His indescribable pain and death on His cross.

For me, emotional pain is the toughest to handle. Feeling isolated can be overwhelming. But we are never alone. Look around you. Yes, you are in pain, but it will end. Look at all those unfortunate souls who live on the street with little to eat and nowhere to go. The world is full of broken people. Why should you be the exception?

God designed the world to be filled with individual choices. We can believe in His words, or not. We can reach out and help others, or not. We can try to become the best version of ourselves, or not. We each can filter out the disorder of the secular world and fill our minds with goodness and hope. It is up to each of us which direction we take in life. Period.

Sometimes offering up our suffering to the Lord helps us work through our suffering. We call this redemptive suffering. It is quite simple; we offer our pain up to the Lord. We recall His great pain on his cross and put our pain in perspective to His. We ask Him to use our pain as the means to move closer to Him. Redemptive suffering was the way of many saints. Many suffered great physical and emotional pain while on earth. Saint Faustina comes to mind.

I think of Saint Faustina when I think about redemptive suffering. She was extremely ill throughout her life, from what is today called tuberculosis. Her attacks started at a young age and continued to greatly affect all aspects of her life. She was wracked with pain. Despite her physical pain, she became a saint. She endured her pain and offered it up to the Lord.

Throughout her life Faustina asked Jesus to accept her suffering as the means to bring her closer to Him. She often could not get out of bed, and her fellow sisters mocked her. Her emotional and physical pain was reflected in many of her diary entries.

Faustina persevered and, through Jesus, gave us the Chaplet of Divine Mercy to receive His unfathomable mercy. Saint Faustina died in pain at the age of thirty-three, the same age our Lord died on His cross.

Some will question the power of the saints, but for me Saint Faustina is an example of true devotion to our Lord. She sets the bar for me on our own ability to fight through our fears, endure the hardships of the world, radiate great faith, and stay in continuous friendship with the Lord.

# Forgiveness

To err is human; to forgive divine. These words are attributable to the English poet, Alexander Pope, in the eighteenth century. When you think about how hard it is sometimes to forgive someone, these words make perfect sense.

Some of us lack the capacity to forgive. We have all met people who actually thrive on their resentments. Resentment fuels their day. They simply cannot let things go. They talk incessantly about how someone has wronged them or bruised their feelings. These people have "hardened their hearts" to the point that they lack the capacity to forgive. Many talk about getting even. They become victims of their resentments and fueled by their anger, they never seem to get off their "pity pots." These people are unhappy with themselves and with life. Sad.

The Lord forgave each of us for our sins and promised each of us a mansion in Heaven, if we followed and obeyed His teachings. Forgiveness is a pillar of Christianity. If we learn to forgive, we are modeling for others a divine virtue. Jesus forgave all of those who asked for His forgiveness. He never held back His mercy for His children.

Most of us will never achieve perfection in this life. Unlike our Blessed Mother, we will sin and fall out of grace with the Lord. But we have a pathway to salvation because of the cross and what He did for us on that cross two thousand years ago. He died so that our sins could be forgiven. This sacrifice was made for all of us to give us hope that, despite our human nature and frailties, each of us have the promise of eternal salvation.

There is one problem with forgiveness, not with God but with each of us. We need to learn to forgive ourselves. Faith is trust. If we trust that the Lord has forgiven us, we need to forgive ourselves and reclaim our lives. As a Catholic, one of the greatest sins you can commit is the sin of denying the power of our Lord to forgive us our sins. Jesus's sacrifice on His cross was the perfect sacrifice and the only one that will ever be needed to ensure our salvation. Like our Blessed Mother, our lives need to be centered around the faith that comes from believing in the promises of her Son.

Don't be too hard on yourself and others. Ease up on those around you who sometimes don't measure up to your expectations. No one is perfect, but we all have the capacity to love, forgive, and show compassion to others. Forgiveness is a gift from God, which we need to model for our friends and family. If you forgive others, you give yourself an opportunity to be grateful. If you are grateful, you are happy.

Don't forget, our Blessed Mother gave us a model for faith, humility, and courage. She never considered herself a victim and always stayed focused on the word of God.

# The End

You cannot undo your life; you can amend it. We come in alone and we go out alone. Death is strictly personal—just you and the Lord.

Many people suffer great terror in their last moments of consciousness. Why? They got it wrong and they realize it in the end. Too late. The clock has stopped. Ask the Lord for His unfathomable mercy. This is your only viable option. The Lord is always with us, and He always listens to our petitions. He was there for the thief on the cross next to him on Calvary. He will be there for all of us, if we let him. Mary will always be there as well. Do not forget she is the Queen of Heaven and has unlimited influence on her Son's mercy. We will all need His mercy in the end.

We recently took a cruise to Ireland, Scotland, and England. I was fortunate to be able to see many wondrous things. We went through many beautiful cathedrals and visited many historic sights. My wife and John's two children, Ayden and Ava, accompanied me on this twelve-day cruise.

Since John died, Dana and I try to stay as close as we can to John's children. Ayden was only nine when he lost his father. Ava was only seven. We take summer vacations with them every year. As they both grow up, we see the image of their father in their faces and in many of their actions. It is healing to our souls to be with John's children. It is a blessing. It is a consolation from the Lord.

As I look back on John's passing and the suffering the family went through, I know it was the Lord's will. John was called home. We all need to remember that God's timeline and actions cannot be comprehended by mortal beings. We need to trust that everything that happens to us in life has a purpose. Like clay, we are all being molded by our Grand Sculptor. God molds us through the trials here on Earth, which we all face. We all have crosses to carry. Some carry their crosses better than others. Every one of us gets wounded in life.

I believe our judgment will be swift and certain. We will see in a flash all our sins, which will be on full display. Jesus Christ will review our life here on Earth and decide our eternal fate. Of course, these are only my thoughts, and you can believe whatever you want about the end of life. I am betting everything I learned from Sister Mary Joseph is true. "Michael, we all need to pray more and have faith in our Lord. It will all work out in the end."

Our meeting with the Creator will determine where we spend eternity. That is a very long time. Like children, we must accept the consequences of our actions. I wish the best for everyone. But a long time ago, I realized that you cannot blame anybody for your mistakes. You have only yourself to blame if you have failed to lead a good life, helped others along the way, and obeyed your conscience and church teachings. Folks, it is that simple.

In the movie *Forrest Gump*, Forrest visits his mother on her death bed. She is dying from cancer. Forrest askes his dying mother, "Momma, what's my destiny? Momma answers,

*"Well Forrest, you are just going to have to find that out for yourself."* Forrest says at the end of the movie, *"I don't know if we have a destiny, or if we are like a feather in the air just floating around. Maybe a little of both."*

We all have a destiny—to be with our Lord in Heaven. In this life, we can help make our own success by studying hard in school, following the rules, working hard, getting along with others, and always asking for help. Some people never seem to make it. My dad would say, "they just fall through the cracks, Michael."

I believe there is a lot of luck in life. Some people can get to the top of their world and achieve fame and good fortune. Most of us struggle from day to day, doing the best we can raising our families, going to work, and enjoying the good times we can spend with loved ones.

We all have tragedy in this life. No one is perfect, and sometimes it seems that we can never win. But we need to keep things in perspective. Yes, life is hard, but the beauty of life outshines the ugliness. In those times of struggle, we need to lean on our faith, especially our Blessed Mother. She endured all the pain of her child's death with dignity and grace. She watched the horror of the crucifixion, but believed in the promise of the Resurrection. She never left her Son's side, and she will never leave our side.

Mary is our greatest example of mortal selflessness, sacrifice, humility, and human dignity. She appears to a few of us periodically. Her message is always the same. Pray to her Son and say the Rosary.

Please don't forget, our Blessed Mother will be there with you in the end to remind her Son about all the good you did with your life. She will remember all the times you came to her when you were suffering and asked for her prayers and intercession. She will remind Him of all the times you helped a stranger or visited a sick friend. Mary will remind her Son about the times you gave a few dollars to the poor and went the extra mile to help out a friend in need. Most importantly, the Virgin Mother will remind her Son of His unfathomable mercy for all of us. These are the simple thoughts that I rely on to keep me focused on my end.

Father Cavana Wallace, one of my former priests, had a nice way of putting things in perspective when talking about Mary:

"Gentleness and patience! These are two qualities Christ experienced firsthand from his mother, Mary, who trusted her Son when He left home and went into the big world to begin His mission. She was not afraid of sending Him into the world, although she knew in her heart the dangers. She is our mother, too, and likewise sends us out into the world to follow her Son. Be assured that she will always look to her Son to guide the family of the Church. And, like the good mother she is, while we are far from home, she also waits and prays for our safe return in the company of Christ, our Lord, who lives and reigns forever and ever. Amen."

As you age, you theoretically gain wisdom. Some do, some do not. Some people want to be victims and blame the world for all their woes. There has only been one true victim in our world—Jesus Christ. I am not a victim. I can still paddle out on my surfboard in the Pacific Ocean and get a wave or two. I am very grateful for this blessing that has been bestowed on me by God. Most importantly, I am grateful for the gifts of faith and family. If you are grateful, you will be happy in this life. If you consider yourself a victim, chances are you will wallow in self-pity and be unhappy.

I hope my grandchildren will find interior peace as they live their lives. For sure, there will be times when they feel defeated and hopeless. I hope they will turn away from their fears and embrace the strength that comes from faith. I hope they will have trust and turn to our Lord when they feel the effects of despair and desolation. I hope they will appreciate the magnificence of our Blessed Mother and her strength as she suffered at the foot of the cross. My prayer for them is that they will always remain in friendship with our Lord. I hope they will say plenty of Hail Marys.

# Appendix A: Staber Mater Prayer

Note: This prayer was sung as a hymn to Mary and originated in the 13th Century.

At the cross her station keeping,
Stood the mournful Mother weeping,
Close to Jesus to the last.

Through her heart, his sorrow sharing,
All his bitter anguish bearing,
Now at length the sword had passed.

Oh, how sad and sore distressed
Was that Mother highly blessed
Of the sole begotten One!

Christ above in torment hangs,
She beneath beholds the pangs
Of her dying, glorious Son.

Is there one who would not weep,
'Whelmed in miseries so deep,
Christ's dear Mother to behold?

Can the human heart refrain
From partaking in her pain,
In that mother's pain untold?

Bruised, derided, cursed, defiled,
She beheld her tender Child,
All with bloody scourges rent.

For the sins of his own nation
Saw him hang in desolation
Till his spirit forth he sent.

O sweet Mother! font of love,
Touch my spirit from above,
Make my heart with yours accord.

Make me feel as you have felt;
Make my soul to glow and melt
With the love of Christ, my Lord.

Holy Mother, pierce me through,
In my heart each wound renew
Of my Savior crucified.

Let me share with you his pain,
Who for all our sins was slain,
Who for me in torments died.

Let me mingle tears with you,
Mourning him who mourned for me,
All the days that I may live.

By the cross with you to stay,
There with you to weep and pray,
Is all I ask of you to give.

Virgin of all virgins blest!
Listen to my fond request:
Let me share your grief divine.

Let me to my latest breath,
In my body bear the death
Of that dying Son of yours.

Wounded with his every wound,
Steep my soul till it has swooned
In his very Blood away.

Be to me, O Virgin, nigh,
Lest in flames I burn and die,
In his awful judgment day.

Christ, when you shall call me hence,
Be your Mother my defense,
Be your cross my victory.

While my body here decays,
May my soul your goodness praise,
Safe in Heaven eternally.
Amen. (Alleluia)

# Appendix B: Rosary Mysteries

## The Joyful Mysteries

*The annunciation of Gabriel to Mary*

"In the sixth month the angel Gabriel was sent from God to a city of Galilee named Nazareth, to a virgin betrothed to a man whose name was Joseph, of the house of David; and the virgin's name was Mary." (Luke 1:26–27).

*The visitation of Mary to Elizabeth*

"In those days Mary arose and went with haste into the hill country, to a city of Judah, and she entered the house of Zechariah and greeted Elizabeth. And when Elizabeth heard the greeting of Mary, the babe leaped in her womb; and Elizabeth was filled with the Holy Spirit and she exclaimed with a loud cry, 'Blessed are you among women, and blessed is the fruit of your womb!'" (Luke 1:39–42).

*The birth of our Lord*

"In those days a decree went out from Caesar Augustus that all the world should be enrolled. This was the first enrollment, when Quirinius was governor of Syria. And all went to be enrolled, each to his own city. And Joseph also went up from Galilee, from the city of Nazareth, to Judea, to the city of David, which is called Bethlehem, because he was of the house and lineage of David, to be enrolled with Mary, his betrothed, who was with child. And while they were there, the time came for her to be delivered. And she gave birth to her firstborn son and wrapped him in swaddling clothes, and laid him in a manger, because there was no place for them in the inn." (Luke 2:1–7).

*The presentation of our Lord to Simeon in the temple*

"And at the end of eight days, when he was circumcised, he was called Jesus, the name given by the angel before he was conceived in the womb. And when the time came for their purification according to the law of Moses, they brought him up to Jerusalem to present him to the Lord (as it is written in the law of the Lord, every male that opens the womb shall be called holy to the Lord) and to offer a sacrifice according to what is said in the law of the Lord, a pair of turtledoves, or two young pigeons." (Luke 2:21–24).

*The finding of our Lord in the temple after three days*

"Now his parents went to Jerusalem every year at the feast of the Passover. And when he was twelve years old, they went up according to custom; and when the feast was ended, as they were returning, the boy Jesus stayed behind in Jerusalem.

After three days they found him in the temple, sitting among the teachers, listening to them and asking them questions; and all who heard him were amazed at his understanding and his answers." (Luke 2:41–47).

## The Sorrowful Mysteries

*The agony of our Lord in the garden of Gethsemane*

"Then Jesus went with them to a place called Gethsemane, and he said to his disciples, sit here, while I go yonder and pray. And taking with him Peter and the two sons of Zebedee, he began to be sorrowful and troubled. Then he said to them, My soul is very sorrowful, even to death; remain here, and watch with me. And going a little farther he fell on his face and prayed, my Father, if it be possible, let this cup pass from me; nevertheless, not as I will, but as you will." (Matt. 26:36–39).

*Our Lord is scourged (beaten and whipped) at the pillar*

"Pilate released Barabbas to them, but after he had Jesus scourged, he handed him over to be crucified." (Matt. 27:26).

*Our Lord is crowned with thorns*

"Then the soldiers of the governor took Jesus into the praetorium, and they gathered the whole battalion before him. And they stripped him and put a scarlet robe upon him, and plaiting a crown of thorns they put it on his head, and put a reed in his right hand. And kneeling before him they mocked him, saying, Hail, King of the Jews!" (Matt. 27:27–29).

*Our Lord carries the cross to calvary*

"And they compelled a passerby, Simon of Cyrene, who was coming in from the country, the father of Alexander and Rufus, to carry his cross. And they brought him to the place called Golgotha (which means the place of a skull)" (Mark 15:21–22).

*The crucifixion of our Lord*

"And when they came to the place which is called the skull, there they crucified him, and the criminals, one on the right and one on the left. And Jesus said, Father, forgive them; for they know not what they do . . .

It was now about the sixth hour, and there was darkness over the whole land until the ninth hour, while the sun's light failed; and the curtain of the temple was torn in two. Then Jesus crying with a loud voice, said, Father, into thy hands I commit my spirit! And having said this He breathed his last." (Luke 23:33–46).

## The Glorious Mysteries

*The glorious resurrection of our Lord*

"But on the first day of the week, at early dawn, they went to the tomb, taking the spices which they had prepared. And they found the stone rolled away from the tomb, but when they went in they did not find the body. While they were perplexed about this, behold, two men stood by them in dazzling apparel; and as they were frightened and bowed their faces to the ground, the men said to them, Why do you seek the living among the dead? He is not here, but has risen." (Luke 24:1–5).

*The ascension of our Lord into Heaven*

"So then the Lord Jesus, after he had spoken to them, was taken up into Heaven, and sat down at the right hand of God" (Mark 16:19).

*The descent of the Holy Spirit at Pentecost*

"When the day of Pentecost had come, they were all together in one place. And suddenly a sound came from Heaven like the rush of a mighty wind, and it filled all the house where they were sitting. And there appeared to them tongues as of fire, distributed and resting on each one of them. And they were all filled with the Holy Spirit and began to speak in other tongues, as the Spirit gave them utterance." (Acts 2:1–4).

*The Assumption of Mary (body and soul) into Heaven*

"Henceforth all generations will call me blessed; for he who is mighty has done great things for me." (Luke 1:48–49).

*The coronation of Mary as Queen of Heaven and Earth*

"And a great portent appeared in Heaven, a woman clothed with the sun, with the moon under her feet, and on her head a crown of twelve stars." (Rev 12:1).

## The Luminous (Light) Mysteries

*The baptism of our Lord by John the Baptist in the Jordan*

"And when Jesus was baptized, he went up immediately from the water, and behold, the Heavens were opened and he saw the Spirit of God descending like a dove, and alighting on him; and lo, a voice from Heaven, saying, This is my beloved Son, with whom I am well pleased." (Matt. 3:16–17).

*The Wedding at Cana*

"On the third day there was a marriage at Cana in Galilee, and the mother of Jesus was there; Jesus also was invited to the marriage, with his disciples. When the wine failed, the mother of Jesus said to him, they have no wine. And Jesus said to her, O woman, what have you to do with me? My hour has not yet come. His mother said to the servants, do whatever he tells you." (John 2:1–5).

*The proclamation of the kingdom of God*

"The time is fulfilled, and the kingdom of God is at hand; repent, and believe in the gospel." (Mark 1:15)

*The Transfiguration of our Lord*

"And after six days Jesus took with him Peter and James and John his brother, and led them up a high mountain apart. And he was transfigured before them, and his face shone like the sun, and his garments became white as light." (Matt. 17:1–2)

*The institution of the Holy Eucharist*

"Now as they were eating, Jesus took bread, and blessed, and broke it, and gave it to the disciples and said, take, eat; this is my body." (Matt. 26:26–30)

# Appendix C: Blessed Mother Prayers

May I always rejoice in your saying yes to the angel Gabriel.

My Lady, guard me against the assaults of the Evil One.

Mother, fill our hearts with compassion and peace.

Mother most chaste and pure, protect me from all doubt and anxiety.

May I be continually reminded of your love for your Son and how you shared His pain at calvary.

Mother Mary, give me the courage to face my fears and stay in friendship with your Son, especially when I suffer from desolation.

Oh Mother of Sorrows, see my suffering here on Earth and gently caress my soul as I wear my pain.

Mother, help us grow closer to your Son in all ways. May our prayers to you be amplified and answered by your most powerful Son.

If all abandon me and I lose hope, may you pick me up, Mother, and hold me close to your Immaculate Heart.

When we are filled with despair, come to us dear Mother, to smooth out the wrinkles in our lives.

At the moment of death, come to me dear Mother, and guide me safely home to your Son.

When I am overcome with fear, fill me with hope, dear Mother.

May we never forget your suffering, dearest Mother. Be with us in our moments of trial, and safely lead us home to your Son.

When I am filled with despair, may I reflect on your suffering at the foot of the cross.

Virgin Mother, pray for us that we may have the courage to amend our ways and enter through the narrow door.

May I reflect upon your magnificent beauty and embrace your Immaculate Heart with complete devotion.

Mother Mary, protect the little ones here on Earth from all corruption and harm.

May Our Lady of the Rosary hear our prayers and bring peace to our hearts and souls.

Oh model of obedience, keep our paths straight and guide us home to the loving arms of your Son.

Speak to your Son and let him know that although I am broken, I trust in His unfathomable mercy.

Mother, may I suffer with dignity always relying in the promises of your Son.

Intercede for me, dear Mother, and ask your Son to hear my most fervent prayers.

Mother of humility and grace, keep us focused on our salvation.

Dear Mother, may I never stray off the path of righteousness, with you at my side to guide me safely home in troubled times.

Our Lady most chaste, pray for my children and grandchildren, that they stay close to your Son. Mother most pure, keep our children close to your Immaculate Heart.

# Appendix D: Fatima Apparitions

Our Lady appeared a total of six times to the children at Fatima, as outlined below:

The first Marian apparition of Fatima, May 13 1917: Mary asked the children to return on the 13th of each month for 6 months. Mary told the children they will suffer much, but will reach Heaven. She then asked the children to say the Rosary every day, to bring peace to the world.

The second Marian apparition of Fatima, June 13 1917: Mary asked the children to add the Fatima prayer (the one above) to the end of each decade of the Rosary. They asked for her to take them to Heaven and she replied, "Soon I will take Jacinta and Francisco, but Lùcia is to stay a while longer." Both children died very young from the Spanish Influenza. Sister Lùcia died at age ninety-seven.

The third Marian apparition of Fatima, July 13 1917: Mary showed the children a vision of Hell and revealed that God wishes for there to be a great devotion to her Immaculate Heart, in order to save souls from Hell. She then predicted the Second World War and the persecution of the faithful in Russia. Our Blessed Mother warned that without prayer and the consecration of Russia to her Immaculate Heart, "Russia would spread her errors throughout the entire world, which would result in more war and the further persecution of the Church."

The fourth Marian apparition of Fatima, August 19 1917: The local administrator imprisoned the children to prevent them from making their meeting with Mary. Six days later, Mary appeared to them in a pasture and asked them to, "Pray, pray very much and make sacrifices for sinners. For many souls go to Hell because there is no one to pray for them."

The fifth Marian apparition of Fatima, September 13 1917: A crowd witnessed white rose petals falling from the sky and then disappearing, as Lùcia asked Our Lady of Fatima to cure the sick. Mary replied that only some would be cured, and that the Lord "has no confidence" in those who were not healed.

The sixth Marian apparition of Fatima, October 13 1917: About 70000 people witnessed "The Miracle of the Sun," from up to ten miles away. News reporters present for the miracle reported an "unexplainable phenomenon." After a stiff rain, the sun came out and actually bounced around in the sky. At one point it looked like it was going to crash to Earth, but then it rose again. At this apparition, Mary revealed herself as the "Lady of the Rosary" and told the children, "People must amend their lives, ask forgiveness for their sins, and not offend our Lord anymore, for He is already too much offended."

# Author Bio

Mike is a retired Marine Corps officer who commanded units from platoon to regimental level from 1972 through 2000. Upon retirement, he pursued a second career in education and has taught classes from the elementary through graduate school levels. All his writing projects (four previous books) are directed towards providing his readers with the essential character and spiritual traits necessary to achieve inner peace in our very secular, chaotic world. He has written extensively about his own life and the impact his leaders, in and out of uniform, have had on his own character development. Mike's real-life experiences with personal tragedy have led him to rediscovering the importance of his faith and the necessity to impart in others a sense of faith and hope, especially in today's world which sometimes seems to be completely disordered. Raised Catholic, this book was written specifically to introduce and reacquaint Christians with the magnificence of the Virgin Mary. The Blessed Mother can be a source of great inspiration to people of all faiths. Mike's hope is that his eight grandchildren and all children will discover the power of faith and the love our Blessed Mother has for each of us. Mike resides in Oceanside, California with his wife of fifty years, Dana.